Poverty & Despair
vs.
Education & Opportunity

Breaking Down the Barriers
&
Building Bridges

Albert M. Colella, Ph.D. and Joseph H. Crowley

Poverty and Despair vs. Education and Opportunity:
Breaking Down the Barriers & Building Bridges

By

Albert M. Colella, Ph.D.
& Joseph H. Crowley

```
Publisher's Cataloging-In-Publication Data
(Prepared by The Donohue Group, Inc.)
Names: Colella, Al. | Crowley, Joseph H.
Title: Poverty & despair vs. education & opportunity : breaking down
    the barriers & building bridges / Al Colella and Joseph H. Crow-
    ley.
Other Titles: Poverty and despair vs. education and opportunity
Description: First Stillwater River Publications edition. | Gloces-
    ter, RI, USA : Stillwater River Publications, [2016]
Identifiers: LCCN 2016932200 | ISBN 978-0-692-63313-7 | ISBN 0-692-
    63313-8
Subjects: LCSH: Poverty--United States--Prevention. | Poor children--
    Education--United States. | Equality--Economic aspects--United
    States. | United States--Economic conditions--21st century.
Classification: LCC HC110.P6 C65 2016 | DDC 339.460973--dc23
```

Some men see things as they are and ask why. Others dream things that never were and ask why not.

~George Bernard Shaw
(paraphrased by **John F. Kennedy** on June 28, 1963)

The world is a dangerous place, not because of those who do evil, but because of those who look on and do nothing.

~Albert Einstein

Dedication

T he efforts and 'message' of this book are dedicated to those individuals, groups, organizations et al that have labored, tirelessly and faithfully, to alleviate those poverty-driven inequalities that have long caused damage and degradation to the humanity and quality of life of those living in poverty. This dedication especially includes those many 'voices' over the many years that have acknowledged this extremely costly situation and have advocated that "something must be done" and have worked toward that goal.

The authors also wish to provide a *special dedication to those individuals -- especially the children and their families --* who have lived under the yoke of poverty and have never really had the opportunities afforded to most other Americans.

Poverty & Despair vs. Education & Opportunity finds its genesis, inspiration and motivation in the lives and efforts of all those cited above. This book really stands upon their shoulders!

If I have seen further,
it is by standing on the shoulders of giants.

~Bernard of Chartres, 12th century
~Isaac Newton, in his 1676 letter

A relevant and exemplary note of recognition is due to Pilar McCloud, NAACP of Providence, one of the five recipients receiving the Rosa Parks Award at the recent [2015] Freedom Fund Gala in Providence, who so eloquently stated

A great way to keep a people oppressed
is to not educate them.

The spirit of this quotation speaks to the dynamic relationship between poverty and education as does this book!

Both authors have been life-long recipients of their experiences with more than a few [quiet] giants within their respective lives.

Personal Dedications

For my mother, Florence, who found herself raising nine children with, during most of those years, an alcoholic husband who though steadily employed preferred to spend many of his days and nights in a bar leaving her struggling with nine children and trying to buy food and pay the rent on what was left of his paycheck after the beer and cigarettes. Not to mention the situations that arose when he came home drunk at 1:00 a.m. All this and, God bless her, when told that she had but hours to live responded, "Well, I've had a good life."

~Joseph H. Crowley

* * *

Recalling the many shoulders -- some known and some unknown to me -- upon which I have stood during my life's journey, I came to an increasingly greater recognition and understanding of the roles that they played within my life. From my young boyhood through my current senior years, I have been blessed with so many quiet advocates who, individually and collectively, have shaped both my inner and outer personae.

Although my early years were spent in a low-income family living in a cold-water flat, I always felt and believed that 'life is good'. However, I also was the recipient of the gifts of advocacy, attention, the love of my Mom and Dad and older brother, encouragement, emotional support, faith, guidance, opportunities for responsibility, helping others [now known as outreach, community service and ministry]

iii

and, especially, the family focus upon the importance of an education and more. My reservoir of gifts grew as the shoulders of so many others lifted me and guided me along my path of life, e.g., teachers, a high school principal, coaches, military comrades, professional colleagues and an army of students over five decades.

It is those shoulders and those gifts that provided the inspiration and motivation to 'make a difference' by writing, along with my co-author, *Poverty & Despair vs. Education & Opportunity*. 'Life is still good!' and my co-author and I wish to pay that forward.

~Albert M. Colella, Ph.D.

Prologue

There appears to be two avenues to addressing the issue at hand. One is moral indignation and an effort to elicit moral indignation followed by a moral mandate to *'do something about poverty.'* The other is a systems oriented, pragmatic approach which says simply: poverty hurts us all and there are ways of stopping that hurt. Over the years, many years, there are many who have cried out in moral indignation with limited results. There are not many, at least not many reaching a wide audience, who have pragmatically documented how poverty costs all of us -- not only the poor -- and that investments for the elimination of poverty have the potential for significant returns on that investment [ROI].

Calls for moral indignation and a follow on moral mandate will be well heard and endorsed by the 'choir'. They may well be totally ignored by those who really and subtly believe poverty is a problem for the poor, the poor's problem to resolve on their own and the rest of us don't have any skin in the game.

In her own words...

A 'voice' of compassion, commitment and hope for all the children -- especially those living in the world of poverty-driven-inequalities!

"I have had the honor and pleasure -- indeed, the experience -- of reading *Poverty & Despair vs. Education & Opportunity: Breaking Down the Barriers & Building Bridges* by Albert M. Colella and Joseph H. Crowley. This book is a much needed enlightenment and awareness of the many dimensions of living in poverty and an inspiration and motivation for action. Additionally, the authors address the spectrum of poverty-induced-inequalities that directly and severely damage the humanity of those who find themselves within poverty's clutches often for reasons and circumstances beyond their control. Poverty deprives many of the quality of life and opportunities always assumed to be an American right.

It is important to note that the authors have provided a systemic perspective into poverty and its unsustainable costs to all Americans -- costs in considerable dollars but costs that go well beyond dollars. Their focus is upon the relationship between poverty and the impediments it creates for the education of children living in poverty and the resultant damage to their quality of life. Ironically, there is reason and rationale that education is the road -- perhaps, the only road -- out of poverty. As expressed by the authors, the road out of poverty goes through the schoolhouse door.

The readers may ask "Why, my voice?"

Simply put, your voice needs to be added to the many 'voices' that have cried out for compassion, commitment, hope and action for decades. I certainly agree with the authors to acknowledge the many efforts that have been brought to bear upon the 'symptoms' of poverty. However, it is equally appropriate to acknowledge the continuing persistence of poverty and its inequalities despite these efforts! The social, economic and humanitarian impact of poverty remains an anomaly in America -- the land of opportunity -- and will remain so until a national goal, priority and commitment of resources for the elimination of poverty becomes a reality.

Returning to the question of "Why, my 'voice'?" in particular? I feel it is my social, civic and moral responsibility to speak out for those without a voice. I am a citizen, a woman, a mother, a grandmother, a Latino and an active member of my state legislature. My life began in very humble beginnings that were economically 'poor' but, fortunately for me, rich in family advocacy, support and belief for the absolute necessity of education. My mother with just a few early grades of schooling was and remains the inspiration for my life and, through me, for my children and my grandchildren. It was my mother's inspiration that motivated me to establish a children's day care center in the inner city for children disadvantaged by poverty. Beyond my family and my community, I entered the political arena as an elected state representative in 2004 where I remain motivated by my mother's inspiration for education.

The authors have provided a forceful and inspiring message for all Americans!"

Grace Diaz
Grace Diaz
Citizen
State Representative
Deputy Chair, Commission on Health, Education and Welfare Chair, Permanent Legislative Commission on Child Care

In his own words...

Thoughts on the 1960s: the Apollo Program and the Great Society. What government can accomplish when leadership clearly identifies a problem and funds its solution.

"The 1960s witnessed two significant challenges that the United States undertook: the race to the moon and the bold social experiment, the Great Society and the War on Poverty.

I was a twenty-four old systems engineer in the summer of 1965. Looking back some fifty years, I recall my impressions of the time especially of the Great Society.

Government, with the peoples' backing, accomplished the most challenging technical feat to this day; it had significant setbacks and was expensive. Back then, I thought that the same approach might be taken with the systemic poverty and inequality in parts of our society. I thought, with a concentrated effort, it might be done in one generation [20 years]. That was fifty years ago!

Albert M. Colella and Joseph H. Crowley bring to the table a system engineer's perspective and mindset to complement their long commitment to those trapped in the poverty-inequality cycle. This book introduces system engineering disciplines to the ongoing battle against the inequalities derived from systemic poverty. It will be an important addition to the armamentarium.

Some added perspective: on May 25, 1961, shortly after the Soviets sent cosmonaut Yuri Gagarin into orbit and returned him, President John F. Kennedy set the challenge of sending men to the moon and returning them safely home by the end of the decade: *a clearly defined goal and timeline.*

On May 7, 1964, President Lyndon B. Johnson introduced the Great Society at Ohio University in a speech " ...and with your courage and your desire, we will build a Great Society... where no child will go unfed and no youngster unfed."

I joined the Apollo Program in January 1963, working on Saturn V booster test instrumentation at the NASA-Michoud facility in New Orleans, LA. I was at the Manned Spacecraft Center, Houston, TX, at the time of the Great Society speech which held so much promise. I was a Lunar Module [LM] Telemetry Systems Integration and Test Engineer.

The 'Moon Program' was the apogee of the systems engineering approach in that imbedded its key elements:

- State the mission and direction
- Investigate alternative approaches
- Model the systems [s]
- Integrate lower level components
- Launch the systems [s]
- Assess performance
- Re-evaluate continually through the life of the mission

These are the same elements imbedded in the systems methodology that the authors have put forth so that the 1964 War on Poverty may, finally be won.

The Apollo Program included a number of necessary steps prior to the liftoff of Apollo 11 and its successful round-trip to the moon. Some of these steps included the Mercury and Gemini Programs and, of course, Apollo missions 7-10.

Apollo 11 fulfilled the commitment of JFK on July 25, 1069 when Apollo 11 splashed down in the Pacific Ocean. There were still five months left in the decade.

It is refreshing to see that the authors are recommending a pilot program as the 'next' first step... prior to proceeding to the 'next' first step, i.e., building upon proven success rather than promise."

William Colleran

Table of Contents

Chapter I
Executive Summary

- Poverty [inner city and elsewhere] and its spectrum of inequalities are ***unfair, undeserved, unnecessary and unacceptable!***
- Shameful situation persists/worsens despite myriad efforts.
- One can only ask the question: "Why?"
- Inner city and other poverty populations are complex and convoluted, very multifunctional and multidimensional 'networks' that have been forged over many decades.
- Most solution-intended efforts have not fully accounted for the impact of crucial 'network' linkages/relationships amongst the many entities that constitute the world of poverty.
- These linkages are not 'linear,' i.e., simplistic cause-and-effect relationships, but are mostly 'nonlinear,' i.e., complex, hidden, unidentified and laden with discontinuities and unexpected cause-and-effects.
- The ***more crucial functions*** amongst the many entities in this complexity of networks are *'poverty'* and *'education'* and their relevant *'linkages'*; their representations [aka models] are developed to demonstrate the intrinsic benefits of a much-needed systemic perspective. To complement the text and 'message' of this book, the transitions from each of these two dominant core functions of 'poverty' and 'education' to a more systemic, complete & comprehensive

representation are provided via a user-friendly website: ***Poverty-Inequalities.com.*** The book does look back to understand the development of the arena of poverty, provides an assessment of the current outcomes of living in poverty and offers a promising perspective of what could be in their future. In order to keep pace with changes in society, government and technology, ***Poverty-Inequalities.com*** has been designed to be a continuously updated complement to the book. Additionally, the interactive function of the website will enable readers of the book and the users of this website to provide inputs, critiques and commentary as appropriate.

- Poverty, as noted, is an extremely complex situation in and of itself and its impact upon society, the rest of us, is equally complex as well as ***costly in dollars and devastating to the humanity and quality of life*** of those living in poverty. Are the poor poor because they are uneducated or are they uneducated because they are poor? Does living in poverty lead the poor to make seemingly, to the rest of us, unwise choices... or... is there something implicit in poverty impacting the brain's executive function? What are the implications of removing a family from poverty conditions through supports, education or a combination of both? Does the nexus between preschool and incarceration justify spending money on preschool? What about other educational programs which lead to improved learning outcomes, graduation rates, post-secondary studies and other non-traditional but emerging educational arenas? Interesting and relevant questions that need to be addressed; this book is a step in that direction!

- A systems approach to studying the poverty-education relationship supports and enables analyses of all the implications of poverty-both on the poverty stricken and on the society in which they live. The systems approach makes a clear case that large poverty populations drain the resources of the middle class. A systems approach belies the oft heard, "If the poor would only pull themselves up by their bootstraps, they wouldn't be poor." Most poor do not even know what bootstraps are and, even if they did, probably could not afford them. A systems approach connects poverty with the taxing of our medical support resources, overburdening our courts and jails, making large urban areas unsafe et al. *A systems analysis clearly points to poverty being a cancer within the total American social system -- a cancer which devastatingly impacts those in poverty and which metastasizes throughout all of society.*

- A systems lens/perspective/methodology will likely yield some distinct advantages, e.g.,

    [1] Provide a distinctly greater 'awareness' of the *rapidly growing and very unsustainable-costs* in terms of $$, opportunity, humanity and the quality of life *afforded to most Americans but not all!*

    [2] Serve as the foundation, context, template, landscape and understanding and reference for the design, development and, when in real-world operations, the relevant plans, strategies and policies *'necessary and sufficient'* to enable durable, cost-effective, meaningful site-specific solutions.

    [3] Representation/model hierarchy, granularity, utility and scalability enable applications in local, state and and national arenas. This application process has its genesis in pilot project[s] that confirm feasibility and provide *verification and validation.*

    [4] Provide a *decreasing* trend in those $$ so often spent inefficiently and ineffectively for poverty populations.

[5] Actually generate a continuing and increasing wide-based *'profit,* i.e., a collateral but significant *increase* in the availability of productive $$.

[6] Reduce the 'costs' to one's humanity and dignity [*consider them to be 'priceless'*] as well as the litany of foregone opportunities so readily and historically available to some -- but not all.

[7] Have the collateral potential to leverage/integrate and, therefore, enhance the 'added value' of the rich spectrum of efforts and results of past and on-going endeavors.

[8] A systems lens will avoid those pitfalls of performance generalities, e.g., efficient, effective, fast, optimal, better, affordable, good response times, adaptive..., ad infinitum.

These general terms are <u>not</u> measures of performance but really potential 'areas of interest'. A systems approach includes both qualitative <u>and</u> quantitative measures of performance. Once the performance areas of interest are verified and validated [hopefully by both the operational managers <u>and</u> users], it is only then that analytical efforts are brought to bear to develop measurable and relevant quantitative measures of performance. The importance of the necessity for metrics is addressed through the text, model development and, especially, on *Poverty-Inequalities.com.*

- The very crucial dynamic relationship between poverty-driven inequalities and the total educational arena is also addressed in detail. Particular attention is focused upon the dynamics of *'learning readiness,' 'teaching readiness'* and the resultant *'classroom management requirements.'*

- It is critically important to note that the ***transition*** and **achievement** of the ***goal for the elimination*** of the 'spectrum of poverty-induced inequalities' [and their *'real' and unsustainable* collateral costs] so long experienced by those in the inner cities and all poverty populations will take time... perhaps, decades... perhaps, longer. However, it is important to note that a target date for goal achievement be mandated within the first five years of the noted transition. One can recall that President John F. Kennedy set the target date for the very ambitious goal of placing a man on the moon; the goal to ***eliminate poverty*** is no less ambitious!

  > One might also recall that the response to the 'civil rights naysayers' of the 1960s was aptly provided by Hubert H. Humphrey: "There are those who say to you - we are rushing this issue of civil rights. I say we are 172 years late." The spirit of this message is equally applicable to those who are reluctant -- for whatever reason -- to move forward in the direction of a solution that reduces/minimizes the impacts of the inequalities of poverty. Simply stated ***'remove poverty and you remove its inequalities.'***

- What are the options as seen via the lenses of humanity, dignity, compassion and 'the right thing to do'? Another way of saying the same thing: "What would you want to be done if you -- or your children -- were a resident of the poverty arena?"... or... as the father of a South Bronx family, when asked "What it was like to live in inner city poverty?" He paused for a few minutes and responded "It's like living in a dark room; you want to get out; you don't know how and no one will show you the way!" The same is applicable to all those families and children within the strata of poverty!

5

- However, if that lens is not readily available, try the LCC [Life Cycle Costs] budget lens which provides a long-term view of those $$ that will likely become available for the American economy and the quality of life of those now living in poverty and, then, those additional $$ even more likely saved via a decreasing spending profile for the costly and devastating inequalities of inner city and poverty residence. ***The incorporation of the proven benefits of LCC budgeting into the efforts to <u>eliminate poverty</u> is an important recommendation by the authors!*** This recommendation is addressed both within the book and on **Poverty-Inequalities.com**. The current budget perspective, practices, protocols and principles also send a very relevant and subliminal message:

  "Pay me now or pay me [more, much more] later!"

- The topics and benefits of
  [1] a 'systems' perspective,
  [2] model hierarchy, granularity, utility and scalability and
  [3] life cycle costs [LCC] are addressed in greater detail in
    supportive Appendices A, B and C, respectively.
- Another question: "Business as usual… or…?
- Amongst the enormous reservoir of ideas, comments, criticisms, theories, beliefs, speeches, writings et al -- some very relevant, some quite solution-irrelevant -- there exists a 'virtual vacuum' of credible, comprehensive and far-reaching plans. Such plans are the inevitable derivative of the systemic view. The words of Dr. Martin Luther King, Jr. capture this thought in his response to some naysayers, e.g., "What is 'your' plan? What is 'your plan' to crush the tragic walls separating the wealth and comfort of the outer city from the despair of the inner city?" **[R1]**

- *This book also addresses [1] a candidate very necessary 'first step' [aka a 'pilot program or 'testbed'] for the proof of the feasibility of a systems methodology and, then, its verification and validation. Having said that, the 'pilot program' would include assessment metrics and their data acquisition requirements for the systemic planning process toward candidate sustainable, meaningful, enduring and cost-effective solutions.*

- A comprehensive, meaningful, high-utility and credible 'systemic' perspective is required to encapsulate these functions and their complex networks of linkages and their relationships. This perspective can yield a credible model and representation for purposes of understanding, analyses of specific poverty sites and a foundational stepping stone to candidate solutions.

- Imbedded within a system perspective is the focus upon credible and meaningful solutions rather than a focus upon the 'symptoms' of the core problem and reasons for the 'headline grabbing' symptoms in the educational arena and more recently, e.g., the recent 'events' in Ferguson, Cleveland, Baltimore, etc.

- Another [potential] collateral outcome of the systemic methodology described in this book may very well motivate, inspire and enable others confronted by seemingly complex situations to take a view through the systemic lens.

Chapter II
Introduction/Background

The book, *'Let's Start with the Children'*, [R2], addresses the development and persistence of the tragic realities, i.e., poverty and the wide range of inequalities and disadvantages, of inner city residence in the South Bronx and its lasting collateral damage to the quality of life, humanity, dignity and the opportunity of residents there -- *especially the children*. Indeed, this situational shame is readily applicable to all the inner cities of America as well as all other areas of poverty, e.g., non-inner city areas, Appalachia and those areas with American Indians and Alaska Natives, that are poverty-stricken and to most of the residents therein. This situation -- in spite of myriad well-intended and alleviating efforts -- has persisted over many decades and still remains unequivocally **unfair, undeserved, unnecessary and unacceptable!** This situation -- this journey for African Americans -- has its genesis in the slave-trade years, e.g., [R3], more than several hundred years ago. Today's inner city poverty situation, for a variety of reasons, was really 'forged' over the many decades that followed as were others areas of poverty. That journey has certainly been a most difficult one for millions of African-Americans; as Dr. Martin Luther King, Jr. reflected in 1958 'We have come a long, long way but we have a long, long, l-o-n-g way to go!" [R4]. This arduous journey [to say the least] continues today and now embraces, not only African-Americans, but also the rural poor, Hispanics, Latinos, Asians, American Indians, Alaska natives, immigrants, a growing number of the middle-class who have been economically marginalized and more. The passage of time has often allowed a willing and convenient denial, tolerance and 'forgetfulness' of the unpleasantness, inhumanity and cruelty of individuals, groups and organizations upon other members of the human race.

There are numerous clichés about 'history repeating itself' and its inferred acquiescence; however, history does *not* have to continue to repeat itself.

There are more contrasting and relevant clichés, e.g., 'what we don't acknowledge, we cannot fix', 'what is the right thing to do?', 'freedom and justice for all', etc. The importance of remembering our history -- all of it and not just convenient selections -- has been addressed by more than a few individuals in education, government, and humanitarian circles, e.g., Simmons [R5]. Another exceptionally 'loud and clear' voice for decades is the continuing efforts of the Children's Defense Fund and, especially the Child Watch Column [R62], Marion Wright Edelman]. These [weekly] website articles provide a very relevant historical and contemporary linkage, i.e., a very necessary component to the understanding of the current inner city/poverty/educational situation for African-Americans with a very collateral applicability to other poverty populations. This countering perspective of remembrance and responsibility by the 'voices' of many over the years is slowly -- ever so slowly -- motivating 'we the people' in the direction of a full justice and social, moral and humanitarian responsibility. One might even feel that this tide will inevitably rise and lift all and not just some!

Over the decades since the costly Civil War and the Emancipation Proclamation, the migration of those African-Americans from bondage to their expectation of 'freedom' provided the background and foundation for the continuing development and persistence of the imbedded disadvantages of poverty, debilitating inequalities, racism and inner city residence that were to follow, [R6-R13]. The Foreword by Gunnar Myrdal and the Introduction to an Epilogue by William Julius Wilson of *Dark Ghetto*, [R14], are particularly illuminating about the inner city environment and the challenge of 'understanding' that environment. The chapter titles provide an incisive itinerary of this book's journey: The Cry of the Ghetto, The Invisible Wall, The Social Dynamics of the Ghetto, The Psychology of the Ghetto, the Pathology of the Ghetto, Ghetto Schools-Separate and Unequal, The Power Structure of the Ghetto, Strategy for Change and Black and White: The Ghetto Inside. This journey still continues today! The monumental Civil Rights and Voting Rights Acts, in spirit and intent, were finally brought to fruition primarily to further level the playing field for African-Americans. However, much more work remains outstanding as so very aptly and comprehensively expressed by James T. Patterson in *Freedom Is Not Enough, The Moynihan Report and America's Struggle over Black Family Life from LBJ to OBAMA* [R15] and others. The message initiated by the United States Constitution, recalled by Abraham Lincoln, fueled by the likes of Dr. Martin Luther King, Jr. and echoed by the Presidential voices of John F. Kennedy and Lyndon B. Johnson and others, again, was 'liberty for all'. These steps forward were clearly necessary legislation and long overdue but not wholly sufficient despite the steadily increasing number of the many supportive 'voices' of advocacy.

Those expectations of freedom and liberty were essentially unfulfilled then, largely unfulfilled during the decades that followed and, sadly and shamefully, really remain unfulfilled for those multi-ethnic millions now living in poverty in the inner cities and elsewhere and beyond their 'virtual walls' of the inner cities of America. This unacceptable -- even convoluted -- situation was and remains debilitating to their humanity, dignity, quality of life and the American promise of equality and opportunity so firmly and clearly imbedded within the United States Constitution.

This situation has been addressed by some, but not enough, courageous and hopeful 'voices' that provided a much needed voice and some measure of hope for those who had little 'voice' of their own. Additionally, that collateral and continuing malaise of 'blindness to humanity' provided relatively few real listeners to their voices.

However, the courageous 'voices' of some who did listen with compassionate and hearty souls, e.g., Abraham Lincoln, Eleanor Roosevelt, Daniel Patrick Moynihan, Dr. Martin Luther King, Jr., Hubert Humphrey, John F. & Robert F. Kennedy, Rosa Parks, John Lewis, James T. Patterson, Peter Edelman and a host of others have, collectively, provided nothing less than a moral mandate for the 'torch of freedom, equality and compassion' to be passed on to current and future generations. Other lesser known individuals and groups, armed only with faith, compassion and commitment as well as little or nonexistent budgets, were also listening and they did and continue to 'answer the call' to their humanitarian duty -- indeed, *a humanitarian and moral mandate* -- they have long been active in the trenches of poverty. It is certainly somewhat ironic that so many efforts are made by those with relatively little power and authority and even less budget; conversely, relatively so few efforts by those located in the chairs of power, budget and authority. Perhaps, *Profiles In Courage* by John F. Kennedy [R17] may offer some information, inspiration and incentive for the latter group. However, *'Let's Start with the Children'* [R2] is one of myriad modest but very effective such efforts of the former group. George H. W. Bush, in his 1989 inaugural address, referred to these many-often unacknowledged efforts -- as '1000 points of light' across America working diligently in the trenches of poverty and other areas of need. He emphasized some very well-earned and well-deserved descriptors for so many who responded to the call for humanitarian duty; he mentioned 'duty,' 'sacrifice,' 'commitment,' and 'patriotism.' Actually, there are probably more than 10,000 [or more] 'points of light'. Another poignant and sustained effort of so many 'in the trenches' that recognizes the poverty-induced damage to children is *Horizons for Homeless Children* [R18]; this efficiently and effectively managed group provides some much needed advocacy for both children and their families living in shelters. Still another such effort is that of the *W. K. Kellogg Foundation* [R19] that bring to bear five of the many 'pieces' that will be integrated into a systemic methodology. They are community and civic engagement, racial equity, educated kids, healthy kids and secure families; a systemic perspective will provide expanded definitions for these five 'pieces' and more than a few others to follow.

The above representative examples may lead the readers to reset their mindsets and awareness of two items from the Executive Summary:

[1] The reservoir of efforts and documentation continue to move, albeit slowly, toward the recognition of the need for a systemic approach to the multidimensional poverty populations of America and their spectrum of inequalities, especially the unique and formidable linkage between poverty and educational inequalities and their many derivatives.

[2] Collectively, these same efforts are enabling inputs to that database so necessary for poverty and education model design, development, utility and validation for the foundational launching/search for solutions. The first step may very well be site-specific pilot projects to assess the feasibility and the application of a systemic methodology to other sites. This reinforces the authors' expectations that inclusion and leveraging of [1] will yield an 'added value' to these efforts and related documentation. Inevitably, the malaise of 'blindness to humanity' and the 'inequality spectrum' will be overcome by the light and vision of human kindness, compassion and when necessary and sufficient social, political and humanitarian will and courage, collectively, shape and enable this moral and American mandate. For those who have been denied their inalienable rights, such a development will then open wide

their gateway to the American dream so enjoyed by so many but, sadly, not all!

Authors' comment: We believe it most appropriate and relevant that our conversation with a Vietnam veteran about the tone, intent and message of this book commented *"You know that veterans throughout history have responded, willingly, to the call of 'honor, duty and country;' our belief was that we thought that our commitment to military service was for all Americans. The failure of this country to not fully open the gateway to the American dream and opportunity to all Americans can only be seen* as a disservice to those who, indeed, served!" *Interesting perspective!*

There is an impressive reservoir of relevant, credible literature in the public domain and, as appropriate, some are cited. The cited references could have been a veritable 'endless' list; those cited references were selected for their representation, relevance and accurate reflection of the wealth of available literature. The contents and their respective references of [R1, Cose], [R14, Clark], [R15, Patterson], [R16, Moynihan] and [R21, Edelman] are particularly relevant, inclusive and comprehensive. However, there are relatively few that provide some measure, hint or inference of a systemic perspective. Certainly, Daniel Patrick Moynihan [R16] offered an early [1965] inference of the need for a comprehensive and relevant perspective via his observation that the woes of blacks in the city were "systemic." A more recent publication [R20] provides an updated (2007) perspective of Moynihan's effort; this 2007 publication hints that the inner city/poverty/educational arena is one of several or more dimensions and addresses some of the relevant topics, e.g., the need for a 'systematic study,' the outstanding need for policymakers with political will and commitment and the byproducts [aka 'outcomes' listed in Figure 2 of Section V] of the poverty populations especially the convoluted inner city/poverty arena. These topics are some of the many related topics that are embraced and aggregated within this book. These topics are but a preview of what is to follow, i.e. the integration/aggregation of these topics into a model, a representation of the poverty populations each with its collateral inequalities-especially educational inequality-with its linkage to one's quality of life!

Two recent books that, together, seemed to provide a much needed compact, very credible and comprehensive historical perspective: first, *Freedom Is Not Enough, The Moynihan Report and America's Struggle over Black Family Life from LBJ to Obama* [R15] by James T. Patterson (2010) and, secondly, *Color Blind* [R1] by Ellis Cose (2001) which depicts an interesting humanitarian perspective and, some insight into a solution. Specifically, Cose states that "there is no simple solution" and provides the recognition that the inner city/poverty issue is, indeed, complex; however, that complexity is not an excuse for inaction.

Coincidentally, this complexity and a long-standing lack of a comprehensive solution methodology are integral parts of the theme of this book. However, a more recent publication, *So Rich, So Poor, Why It's So Hard To End Poverty in America* [R21] by Peter Edelman (2012, 2013) stands out as a motivating force for forward motion and also consistently served as an inspiring, incisive and meaningful reference. This very grounded and credible book by Edelman -- one of his many -- also provides a much needed and clear voice for a systemic approach to the inner city/poverty/educational arena issue. His particular voice gives instant and unwavering confirmation and validation of the 'comprehensive solution' thesis on pp. 231 and 232 of *Let's Start with the Children* [R2] and its more detailed argument and advocacy herein.

So Rich, So Poor by Peter Edelman (2013) represents the most detailed and comprehensive awareness and understanding of the 'systemic' phrase touched upon and/or inferred by others. The following phrases from this remarkable -- even iconic -- book certainly convey to the readers some details of a 'systemic approach':

- "we do not see the linkages that tie everything together for an all-points response." [p. 102]

14

- "synergism" [p. 117]
- "multi-dimensional design" [p. 125]
- "education is the cornerstone" [p. 124]
- "issues cannot be confronted one-by-one because everything is connected to everything" [p. 124]
- "integrated part of a larger regional development" [p.131]
- "broader approach" [p.132]
- "collective impact" [p. 136]
- "systemic issues" [p.138]
- "on all fronts" [p. 141]

Edelman's noted very relevant inferences in *So Rich, So Poor,* and a more detailed supporting reason and rationale in Appendix A, Systems Prologue, are provided in order to give to the readers, additional definition, detail, insight into and understanding of these 'phrases.'

Poverty and education models are introduced in Section V, Poverty, Education and Their Linkages, which provides an initial view of system perspectives of poverty and education with examples of their network of 'linkages' within each model. These models, then, become the dominant inputs to the 'cost of poverty' model. It is important to recognize that the costs are more than dollar costs. There are costs to humanity, quality of life, opportunity and more; in forthcoming sections, the poverty-imposed inequalities each have wide-spectrum costs including and beyond dollars. We discovered, during a brief trip to Maine, more than a few references hidden in its many small bookstores. Recently [June 2015], we came across one such reference that has added a few more dimensions of poverty. *The Rich and the Rest of Us, A Poverty Manifesto by Tavis Smiley and Cornel West* [published by Smiley Books in 2012] adds the *poverties of opportunity, affirmation, courage, compassion and imagination.* Sections VI, Poverty Model and VII, Education Model, respectively, provide a significantly enhanced comprehensive view of the Poverty and Education Models each with its network of 'linkages'. This view is additionally complemented via a user-friendly website [***Poverty-Inequalities.com***] that enables the user to explore both models as well as to focus upon specific areas of user interest. The authors submit that these sections, in particular, will provide a broad view of these linkages and their individual and collective devastating impact upon the quality of life of those in the many strata of poverty... and, of critical relevance, the challenge of developing candidate solutions that address these impacts, individually and collectively, as so strongly inferred by Edelman in *So Rich, So Poor.*

Chapter III
Why?

N ow that's a great question! More specifically, like so many individuals with a wide spectrum of interests and perspectives, i.e., concerned and compassionate citizens throughout and across the vertical and horizontal hierarchies of America over the many years and decades, we also asked that often asked question: ***"Why? Why does this unfair, undeserved, unnecessary and unacceptable situation persist for those living in poverty and in the inner cities of America?*** Certainly, there have been myriad efforts since the advent of the 20th century to alleviate this situation. There have been mandated policies, programs and measures from both the Federal, state, city and local governments. For example, see Edelman [R21; pp. 17, 21, 35, 70...] but especially his comment on p. 159, i.e., "So if you look objectively at what has happened, the claim that nothing works is revealed for what it is -- totally hot air." This is really a well-earned and well-deserved tribute to those in public and personal service whose efforts have made a difference to those living in poverty. One very outstanding characteristic of a 'systems' perspective is that it will enable a dramatic synergism amongst the many focused, independent and 'unlinked' efforts. It is an interesting irony that 'so much has been done' yet 'there is so much more to be done'. ***"How can that be?"***

Clearly, the current state of those living in poverty-stricken areas, e.g., the inner cities of America, does present the 'other side of that coin' in that it is also a recognition of the intrinsic complexity of the situation and the sheer enormity of the work that still remains to be done! Putting it another way, it is interesting to note that many presidential candidates for decades have taken photo opportunities amidst the crumbling neighborhoods of the South Bronx [R22] [and, most likely, in other inner cities and, not as frequently in other areas of entrenched poverty] as a necessary part of their respective campaign efforts. Paraphrasing their many colorful promises [with very brief lifetimes], their common message was that something would be done; perhaps this 'message' may have been the 'next step' following Moynihan's 1965 message that 'something must be done'. History and that limited progress cited above and elsewhere have demonstrated the accuracy and falseness of that promise. Nevertheless, taking a walk through any of America's inner cities and other poverty-stricken areas clearly provides overwhelming evidence that there is still much work that does remain and that it will take time... much more time... a long, long time! Perhaps, just perhaps, the complexity, enormity and cost and the time required for 'something to be done' is intimidating, even scary...that is understood! ...however, the aggregate costs of 'looking the other way' have really only 'kicked the can down the road' even as the costs continue to increase and aggregate... it is a bill just waiting to be paid! Sooner or later! And until that happens, a very significant human cost will inevitably be a myriad children falling through that 'enormous crack in that proverbial floor.'

Part of the answer to the original question '*Why?*' probably lies in some understanding of African-American history starting with the slave trade-years and the difficult acknowledgement that the African-American population was forcefully and continuously devalued as humans for hundreds of years. This process-enabled by economics, fear, ignorance and irresponsible acceptance -- evolved into a unique form of hostile, cruel, overt and subtle racism and culture which still exists today. Again, there has been progress but, sadly, although necessary, it **is not** a sufficient 'supply' for the 'demands' for the required progress. Of the available relevant literature **to understand this history**, *More Than Just Race: Being Black and Poor in the Inner City* [R23] provides a research-based view as a context for [1] 'understanding' as well as [2] some of the inner city and poverty inequalities. Another author, political scientist and more, James Q. Wilson, also provides an impressive and informative -- even remarkable -- litany of nearly 300 essays that span more than five decades [1960-2012]. Wilson, an American and political analyst, covers a wide spectrum of topics that span more than five decades [R24].

Other poverty populations, e.g., Native Americans, Appalachia, immigrants, etc., each have 'their own histories' of their respective journeys into and through poverty; each warrant an understanding of their journeys as a prerequisite for the shaping of candidate 'solutions' that are relevant and durable. A recommended starting point is the rich database of authored works, e.g., those of Ruby K. Payne and her team of co-authors. She has authored more than a few books that address the many outcomes and understanding of poverty from 1999 to 2010, e.g., *Bridges Out of Poverty*, 2006 [R26]. Another is *A Framework for Understanding Poverty, 4th Edition*, 2005 [R27]. This particular book could be viewed as an encyclopedia for the many elements, factors, dimensions and reflections of the poverty arena. The topics are relevant and even enlightening for those novice teachers assigned to poor performing schools [usually found in poverty areas]. Topics, e.g., 'hidden rules among classes', may be quite surprising to those novice instructors that have never interacted with those children and families in poverty. There are informative 'case studies', discipline issues, i.e., 'classroom management,' data on different strata of poverty [including deep poverty] and household incomes. It is a useful 'primer' to assist teachers whose first professional assignments may be in low-performance schools with children in poverty. Paine's Research Notes are excellent references.

From September, 2014 to the present time, I have had the opportunity to share a series of discussions with a 2014 graduate with a baccalaureate degree in early education This young lady has an excellent academic background, an innate intelligence and a commitment to 'make a difference'; she comes from a family structure in which education has always been considered a responsibility as well as an opportunity and a necessity for employment, upward mobility, success with regard to both tangible and intangible entities. Her family included several professionals in the academic arena from early education to arenas beyond high school and graduate studies. One would think that this young woman would more than likely experience success in any classroom; she certainly seems to have positioned herself for success in the educational arena.

However, during the past twelve months, we have had some very extensive discussions -- even heated discussions -- about the enormous chasm between her preparation over the years [including college and student teaching assignments] and the challenge within her assigned classroom. Basically, the children were products of low income and dysfunctional environments and their attitudes and behavior were primarily shaped by their environments.

The resultant necessity for *classroom management* surfaced as the greatest challenge within this environment; much of the classroom time -- sometimes the greater part of the classroom time -- is, by necessity, devoted to classroom management. Common sense tells us that when classroom management is being pursued out of sheer necessity, the processes of 'learning' and 'teaching' are significantly compromised. Without additional classroom resources beyond the individual teacher being made available, this becomes an act of futility and the opportunity to 'make a difference' to the children [they are the 'clients'], so sadly, becomes a foregone opportunity!

Whereas she was primarily concerned with the basic educational needs [you know: reading writing and 'rithmetic], the school administrators *seemed* to be unaware of the challenges within the classroom and, more importantly, the resources required to successfully engage these challenges. Rather, they focused upon test scores, grades and other educational metrics that do work in many other classrooms -- especially those *beyond* those in poverty populations. There seemed to be a goal to simply 'move the children along to the next grade' -- *prepared or not!*

Common sense also compels us to provide resources according to the needs, i.e., 'one size doesn't really fit all' [R25]; it is understood that 'one size could fit all' with the conditions that *'learning readiness'* for the children and *'teaching readiness'* for the instructors co-exist within the classroom and, most importantly, have a continuum of advocacy. The 'Readiness' spectrum, model and dynamics are also addressed in greater detail in Section V and its website version in Chapter VII.

Carole Marshall [R28, R29] provides some experiential insight into urban schools with regard to disservice to students, administrative flaws et al; the following statement is noteworthy: "We cannot improve urban education on the cheap. Urban students need more services than their peers elsewhere...." Again, it is important to acknowledge that, educationally, 'one size doesn't fit all'. Lacking such an acknowledgement is an impediment to educationally progress!

Another part of the answer could be the 'pep rally effect' that takes place after a well-known and knowledgeable advocate and 'voice' for progress speaks publicly. There were always many listeners -- actually, sincere listeners -- that also listened to their own resonating goodness and became excited and enthusiastic about joining an effort to make a difference in the lives of others. These listeners -- individuals, politicians, organizations et al typically expressed strong agreement with the 'voice' of an advocate. However, the passage of time often yielded a rapidly diminishing advocacy and involvement by the advocate followed by little activity. There is an abundance of 'voices' using the needs of people as political leverage and rhetoric and not much more. Many 'talk the talk' but relatively few 'walk the walk;' in the 1960s, 'for the vast majority of white Americans, it was a time of struggle to treat the Negro with a degree of decency, not of equality' [Cose, R1]. Cose tells us that 'white America was ready to demand that the Negro should be spared the lash of brutality and coarse degradation, but it had never been truly committed to helping him out of poverty, exploitation or all forms of discrimination. When Negroes looked for the realization of equality, they **found that many**

of their white allies had quietly disappeared.' Simply and directly put, what is needed today is not another pep-rally but rather durable leadership, commitment, a lens for 'humanity', another lens for long-term budgeting and enabling of necessary and sufficient resources!

Colella [R2] reminds us that "The relevance of the goodness model to ministry is that it is the reservoir of goodness -- *when tapped* -- and enabled becomes the sustaining force in the life of any particular ministry. Additionally, in the same sense that *one ministry begets another* so does *goodness beget goodness.* It is both of these two dynamic phenomena that literally release the waters of goodness from the myriad individual, community, corporate and government reservoirs into the arena of need. Just some food for thought! The word, 'ministry', according to Webster, has **numerous definitions or meanings; however,** the common thread inferred in each is really 'service to those in need' in any and all arenas of life, i.e., *no exceptions!* The authors believe that there is goodness in every human being waiting to be discovered, released or enabled; however, society has literally 'buried' goodness and often opted for irrelevant, meaningless and shallow goals.

Returning to the question of *"Why?"* the complexity of the inner city poverty and educational disadvantages start to manifest themselves. Racism that became an imbedded American culture for decade upon decade with an assist from those who practiced denial, irresponsibility, blindness to humanity, hatred et al gave rise to a multitude of derivatives aka 'inequalities'. Simply enacting a law that prohibits racism does not erase the long-imbedded spectrum of inequalities and their costly and devastating outcomes. This spectrum includes racial inequality, humanity inequality, economic inequality, housing inequality, educational inequality, legal and justice inequality, health inequality, upward mobility inequality, opportunity inequality, family structure inequality, life span inequality... 'voice' inequality and more! It is a glaring irony that America has always responded to the 'needs' of individuals, groups, towns, cities... and even countries beyond its shores. As a country, America has a remarkable history of remarkable 'first responders', e.g., responsiveness to the needs of an individual, neighborhood, community in crisis and even a wide spectrum of global needs... disaster relief, World War II, the Marshal Plan, and a litany of relief efforts throughout the America's history certainly come to mind! In contrast to this long established and proud American legacy is the unfinished business of including 'all of its peoples' into the remarkable American dream.

One really doesn't need more factors to expound upon the answer to the question of *'Why?'* but there are more 'pieces' to a more complete answer. Three of the many additional 'pieces' of the answer lie in the intentional and unintentional isolation of areas of poverty, e.g., gentrification [R30], poor urban planning [R31] and 'redlining, i.e., the refusal of home mortgages or home insurance to areas or neighborhoods considered to be poor financial risks by some of America's banks. Many of these and other 'pieces,' in part or in whole, are direct derivatives of racism.

Additionally, financial venture economics and its dynamics are not random events but rather well-planned strategies for a successful 'bottom-line' outcome [aka 'profit']; of course, some of these outcomes are intended to benefit a relatively few regardless of the cost to so many. Specifically, such well-planned financial plans also have other inevitable outcomes that may increase the levels of poverty to those who are in residence in the middle and lower parts of the economic scale. Due to a malaise of 'blindness to humanity' these financial plans have emphasized short-term gains [aka quick 'profits'] for a few rather than some consideration of long-term effects upon the general population -- especially those living in poverty. In 1991, Michael T. Jacobs published **Short-Term America** [R32] which addressed the recklessness of such a 'profits now and let's not be concerned about tomorrow and those we hurt' economic strategy which is readily applicable to the current inner city, poverty and educational crisis. The financial arena in the 1990s and early 2000s provides us with a more recent example of 'short-term' outcomes with disastrous results for millions of Americans due to loss of their homes, their jobs, their family structures, their futures and more. A disaster which continues to this day. One specific very sad result is that more than a few charitable foundations were financially damaged/obliterated in the quest of the 'few' for 'quick' profits. Specifically, this carefully planned 'redistribution of wealth' simply pushed many middle class Americans into the ranks of poverty, increasing the populations of marginal existence, poverty and extreme poverty. Again, reference is made to Edelman's *So Rich, So Poor* [R21]. Does the achievement of a record high of the Dow Jones Industrial Average in July, 2014 in the face of consistent high levels of poverty and an employment strategy that does not provide a 'living wage' [as opposed to the minimum wage] simply a continuation of this noxious 'redistribution of wealth'? Simply take notice of those various 'reasons' and 'suspect rationalizations' that are cast forth to defend that strategy of maintaining the status quo of wages with a significant gap between minimum wages and living wages. Could the real driving force for this strategy be an opting for profits versus fair and humanitarian-based wages?

Let's cite two additional references: first, the very recent appearance of Bernie Sanders, Chairman, United States Senate Committee on Veterans' Affairs, on NBC's *Meet the Press* on September 14, 2014 [R33]. He is an independent and has been a member of the Congress since 1991. His message was simple but very powerful and very much to the point; he considers the American people to be angry about the accumulation of wealth, and, therefore power and authority, in the hands of a 'few' and a steadily decreasing income for more and more…and the gap is growing!

Senator Sanders refers to this trend as a migration toward an oligarchy and, most certainly, away from the principles of democracy, i.e., 'government of the people, by the people and for the people'. Call it a coincidence if you so wish but Bernie Sanders was, again, on Meet the Press on July 26, 2015 {R33A] but as a 2016 candidate for the nomination for the Presidency of the United States. This latter appearance was particularly interesting in that Sanders message to the people about the issues still facing America and the next President remained intact and even more relevant than 2014. It was also more than interesting to observe the Moderator, Chuck Todd, of Meet the Press, employing his usual tactics to steer/shape the conversation for resonance with his own perspective rather than allow Sanders the courtesy of fully expressing his position on several issues. It certainly appeared that the efforts of the Moderator were to inject his own perceived ideas and opinions into the conversation with Sanders. To the credit of Sanders, he maintained his position on each issue and fully rebutted as incomplete and even erroneous perceptions of the Moderator who really looked like he didn't do his 'homework' with respect to Sanders' position on issues.

A second reference -- very relevant to the theme of this position paper -- is *How Business Schools Can Help Reduce Inequality* [R34] by Robert Reich, American political economist, professor, author and political commentator and Secretary of Labor [1993-1997] under President Clinton who also served in the administrations of Presidents Ford and Carter.

Interestingly, this same commentary was also entitled *Harvard Business School's Role in Widening Inequality.* Basically, Mr. Reich provides some additional context for the curriculum, focus and that 'set of ideas and principles' that have widened the pay gap between CEOs and the ordinary worker, e.g., he states that the CEO/worker wage ratio went from 20:1 in 1964 to 300:1 in 2014. The imbedded focus was upon corporate competiveness, i.e., profit without due diligence for the economic impact upon the American workers. This is simply another example of the unfair 'redistribution of wealth' during the last several decades. The education of CEOs is referred to as a substantial social investment but Mr. Reich also questions the social returns on that investment and infers whether these business school graduates are using some of their intellectual and creative capacities for humanitarian purposes. Some food for thought!

It is within this context of economic recklessness and irresponsibility that Life Cycle Costs [LCC], addressed in Appendix C, become a very necessary ingredient into the solution process. Simply put

LCC analysis has long proven to be effective in *determining the 'true costs' of implementing a plan, a product or an action* beyond their initially perceived costs; history is abundant with almost unbelievable examples of steadily increasing 'cost overruns' as time passes.

Even more simply put, the vacuum caused by the omission [often intended] of LCC analyses contributes directly to the inefficiency of the budgeting and performance processes. It is for this reason that Appendix C, *Life Cycle Costs-What Are They? A Necessary Part of the Solution,* **warrants inclusion within this book** as it is a very critical and very relevant component of a systems perspective as well as a real-world necessity. A meaningful 'test' for the inclusion/exclusion of any component is to consider the relevance and impact upon the goals of interest [via extrapolation] of either within a real-world context. Although it may seem a bit dramatic but the failure to integrate/leverage LCC analyses into the solution methodology and process would most likely render the solution outcomes as marginal, at best! Think about it!

The Price of Inequality: How Today's Divided Society Endangers Our Future [R35 (2012)] by Joseph E. Stiglitz, Nobel-winning economist and former Chief Economist of the World Bank provides a more global and perspective of the trends of both social and economic inequality. Book reviews by Case [R36], Edsall [R37] and Blackhurst [R38] offer helpful collateral comments. However, Stignitz also offers an additional and even revealing insight into the most likely real-world reasons and rationale for the growth of two very unequal societies within America in *The Great Divide*: Unequal Societies and What We Can Do About Them [R39 (2015)]. Just as Edelman so succinctly pointed out in 2013 in *So Rich, So Poor*!

There is still another 'piece' of the answer that warrants recognition. In 1992, William J. Bennett gave us *The Fight for Our Culture and Our Children* [R40]. Among his many topics, Bennett makes reference to those individuals who have waged an all-out war on common sense and the common values of the American people. This departure from common sense and values may very well be an intangible, hidden and subtle force but it may also be part of the answer to *'Why?'* Bennett, long active in the activities of the nation's capitol, recalls the advice of his wife, Elayne [also, an author, e.g., [R41]: "...single best piece of advice he received while he was serving in government was to get out of Washington and visit the rest of America!" The views from Washington and many State legislatures really don't include the substance, legacy, needs and responsibilities of America. Increasingly so, the words, acts and actions of these 'democratic' entities seem not only irrelevant but also bordering on the naïve and ridiculous. The relevance of that statement should be obvious to many, if not all; perhaps, a reflection about the political climate in Washington during the last several years may be enlightening!

There are really many 'pieces' to answer that same question; certainly a reflection by John Siegenthaler that appeared in an article in the Miami Herald in May of 2011 written by Leonard Pitts goes directly to the core of the blindness to humanity. In that article, *50 Years Later, A Soul Struggles,* [R42] Siegenthaler recalls 'how could the tragedy of American racism have been so invisible to him and his contemporaries until movements like the Freedom Riders forced them to see'. That blindness malaise still lingers.

Ralph Ellison wrote three books that cover more than three decades: He wrote *Invisible Man* in 1952 [R43], *Shadow and Act* in 1964 [R44] and, in 1986, *Going to the Territory* [R45]. Each of Ellison's three books depicts the life of African-Americans as seen through their eyes, hearts and minds. This blindness by many -- but not all -- to the needs of other poverty populations is also with us!

Barone and Ujifuse [R46] remind us of 'institutional accountability' in the Almanac of American Politics, National Journal, Washington, DC, 1992.

They indicate that 'reclaiming institutions is less a political opportunity than a civic [moral] obligation... a sense of right and wrong.' The factor of 'accountability,' often not fully embraced by some individuals, organizations and agencies is included in the representation/model of the inner city poverty and educational arenas. The following principle holds true: Without accountability, corruption of ideals, actions and goodness will, without question, inevitably become a way of life. It is the most critical factor in any process; history tells us that without it, chaos and irresponsibility will surely prevail. With it, there is hope, opportunity and progress... for all!

History also tells us that there is a time to move from the question phase, i.e., *'Why?'* and its partner. i.e., *'What can be done?'* to the development of a comprehensive strategy [R2, Chapter 20] that enables durable, relevant, equitable [aka 'fair,' 'just,' 'moral'] and effective 'solutions'. Such a development requires

> [1] an 'awareness', i.e., an information-based acknowledgement and understanding of the complexity of the inner city poverty, education, employment, housing, health, crime and criminalization and so much more!....and, secondly,
>
> [2] an informed acknowledgement and understanding of those events, e.g., laws, causes, attitudes and practices [both overt and covert] that shaped the history of poverty areas and enabled the long-term development of poverty both in the inner cities and elsewhere in America. The reason and rationale for [1], simply put, is that 'what is not acknowledged cannot be fixed'; a crucial piece of that acknowledgement is the acceptance of responsibility! The reason and rationale for [2], simply put, is an understanding of the history of poverty [aka 'lessons learned'].

The goal of this book is to address both the 'awareness' requirement *and* an inner city/poverty representation [aka 'model'] that is knowledge-based with respect to the 'history' mentioned above. This 'model' offers a candidate and credible foundation and starting point for the 'next step': the validation of the methodology both necessary and sufficient for the development and updating of relevant, realistic and meaningful 'long-term' solutions as opposed to the 'pep rally' smoke and false promises of 'short-term' solutions. The requirement to determine the feasibility and applicability of a 'solution' is a site-specific pilot program'. This is addressed in Chapter VIII.

Of course, it is an often mentioned theme within this writing that one of the very necessary commitments is the collective national will; this commitment translates, unconditionally, to the need for collective leadership. As a reminder, it may be necessary to delineate the elements of 'leadership':

[1] set the appropriate national goal,

[2] develop a plan/policy/strategy that is goal-oriented and, most importantly,

[3] provide the leadership, the motivation, the inspiration and the resources to the population at all levels. A relative corollary is 'Don't forget the 'clients', the American people, *__all__* the American people!

Chapter IV
Some Necessary Observations

T he cited references in *Poverty & Despair vs. Education & Opportunity: Breaking Down Barriers & Building Bridges* were selected from the virtual reservoir of available documentation because of their, individual and collective, relevance, sufficiency, realism and credibility. It is the authors hope that the reader will develop an awareness of the world of poverty et al via the synergistic effect of these selected references. Each reference is, in fact, an integral part of a larger story; collectively, these references are telling a long-awaited and much-needed 'story.'

It is equally important to note that the cited documentation -- as well as the totality of available documentation -- provides a spectrum of perspectives from the hierarchy of American society. The authors thought it quite remarkable -- even astonishing -- that these perspectives grew in number and relevance from individuals not so well known [R2} as others in the national and media spotlights. These perspectives, these voices, for far too many decades, have not broadly resonated with those with position, authority and, most importantly, responsibility. The continuity, credibility and relevance of those not so well known individuals have reached a critical point, i.e., a societal mandate for action not words.

The authors would be remiss in their responsibility if they do not acknowledge the unique contribution of all reviewed and cited documents to the development and publication of *Poverty & Despair vs. Education & Opportunity.* Their individual and collective contributions are, very respectfully and appreciatively acknowledged. This book is really built upon their shoulders. It simply would not have been possible without their commitment to 'due diligence.' Their efforts, perseverance and 'passion' for social justice are the inspiration, motivation and foundation for this book.

This book, clearly, is not a solution but rather a wake-up call for the awareness and acknowledgement of the growing and soon-to-be *unsustainable* and multidimensional *'real costs'* of poverty and its innate inconsistency with American society as promised and mandated by the United States Constitution. Although not a solution, per se, this book does provide the much-needed context and landscape so necessary for the development of candidate solutions leading to the reversal, minimization and, at best, *the elimination of poverty and its spectrum of inequalities as well as the unsustainable and real costs of poverty!*

The authors' approach to the enormity and complexity of the network of linkages between the many inequalities of poverty, education and the individuals' *quality of life* [as prescribed by the United States Constitution] emphasizes the awareness, acknowledgement and acceptance for America's *unfair, undeserved, unnecessary and unacceptable* environment of the different strata of poverty. Although intended to be enlightening to many and constructive to all, i.e., 'some food for thought', there will be the criticisms of the personal and professional naysayers but there, just as inevitably, will be the constructive comments and critiques of many.

Finally, the authors do respectively understand and acknowledge that the spectrum of topics and cited references will, *initially*, seem to be disjointed but, after some reasonable and reflective thinking, the 'linkages' among the many topics and cited references will be viewed via a 'systemic' lens. Hopefully, this view, reflecting the hopes of the authors, will then give rise to an increased awareness and acknowledgement that *'something must be done'* [R16].

Chapter V
Poverty, Education & Their Network of Linkages

POVERTY and its LINKAGES

J ust for 'starters, so to speak, it is interesting -- even overwhelming -- to have discovered that an internet search for 'inner city poverty programs' yielded more than 10,000,000 'hits;' this extraordinary quantity of available -- and very diverse -- literature reflects that 'poverty' has attracted a lot of attention, perspectives and observations for decade upon decade. It would be a monumental task to 'capture' the available literature in its entirety. However, as mentioned previously, the cited references are significantly reflective of this wide spectrum of the relevant literature.

Poverty is addressed in a variety of forms; measures of poverty usually include some dollar-based measures and an acknowledgement that poverty, per se, creates a multi-dimensional chaos amongst those in residence within the poverty arena. It is not the intent of this book to define poverty using only income dollars as a metric but rather to address the impact of poverty -- and all of its linkages -- upon the overall 'quality of life' of those in poverty. This section will specifically address the many known linkages between 'poverty' and the 'Inequality Spectrum' as well as the linkages amongst the inequalities, per se. As it will be seen, the same argument can be made for the education function; in sections to follow, the reader will see that the education function has its own network of clusters and linkages to the 'Inequality Spectrum'. It is important to acknowledge both the poverty and education networks and, as will also be seen, their dynamic relationship that together are enabling an unsustainable cost.

It is recognized that poverty is not a choice -- as inferred by more than a few -- but rather one's residence in poverty -- for whatever reason -- is primarily due to society's as well as one's own unawareness of options and available choices when 'living in poverty'. Remember that father from the South Bronx [R2] who offered that living in the South Bronx is akin to living in a dark room and not knowing how to get out and, then, there is no one to show him the way. Really a very profound analysis from a client! Also, from [R2] and mentioned earlier in this book, areas of poverty have 'virtual walls' that prevent their residents from those opportunities that exist but are denied to them. We are reminded about recent AOL postings, e.g., Trevor Conley [June 7, 2015] and Natalie Morin [June 3, 2015] entitled 'The other side of the dream -- where poverty exists'. This posting refers to the latest income report from the United States Census Bureau and looks at the 'spread' of the most impoverished counties from 1980 to 2010. This view is another motivating factor for exploring 'roads out of poverty'. This is one of the compelling reasons and rationale for a durable commitment for individuals, families, communities and a national advocacy. It is important to recognize that the 'durable commitment' must be as multi-dimensional as the situations and linkages in poverty-stricken areas.

Having said that, here are some examples from the cited literature: the National Academic Press [R47, 1990] provides a multi-faceted look at inner city poverty; the Malcolm Wiener Center for Social Policy [R48, 1987-1988] addresses urban poverty, family life, joblessness and some poverty research programs; Teitz and Chapple [R49, 1998] present eight urban hypotheses and factors that infer the need for a 'systems perspective.'

More recent treatments of poverty are Breaking the Cycle of Poverty in Young Families **[R50, 2013],** A New Model for Ending Inner City Poverty **[R51, 2012],** Social Solutions to Poverty: America's Struggle to Build a Just Society **[R52, 2007],** Health and Human Services Poverty Guidelines **[R53],** Readings, Lectures No. 1-23, MIT OpenCourseWare, Urban Studies and Planning, Poverty, Public policy and Controversy **[R54, 2003].**

Of course, there are some writings that are so extremely focused [often as a direct derivative of one's 'agenda] that the more relevant 'big picture' [aka a systems perspective] is sacrificed or, perhaps, unacknowledged via the skill of unawareness! Several outstanding examples are provided by Paul Ryan, i.e., [R55, 2014], and his equally misguided update [R57] of July 2014 advocating 'expanding opportunity in America'. The Children's Defense Fund provides a quick and very appropriate response, [R61] and [R57] to both [R55] and [R57]. Then there are those 'voices' that are a refreshing breath of fresh air that call for pilot programs, e.g., [R58], the core indicator efforts of The Annie E. Casey Foundation [R59, 2011] and the parallel efforts of Rhode Island KIDS COUNT [R60]. The latter efforts, acknowledged previously in [R2] pay particular attention to four core cities in which the highest percentage of children are living in poverty.

Specifically, Rhode Island KIDS COUNT's focus upon 67 indicators within five core indicators shaping the quality of life of children: *Family and Community, Economic Well-being, Health, Safety* and *Education.* The authors consider [R18], [R19], [R47] - [R52], [R53], [R54] and [R62] as outstanding contributions to an enhanced and enlightened understanding that one's 'quality of life' is, very much multidimensional, and are in strong resonance with the need to consider a 'systems methodology' as a prerequisite for the development and assessment of candidate multidimensional solutions responsive to poverty-driven inequalities.

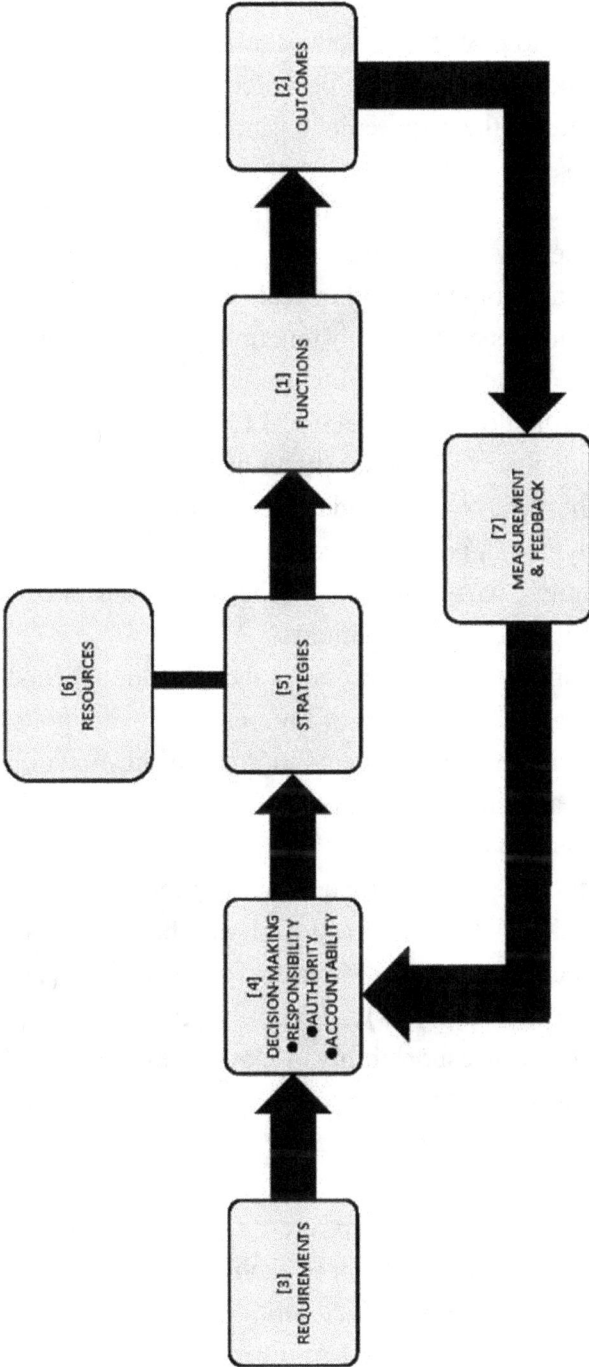

FIGURE 1 - CANONICAL FORM/MODEL FOR ANY SYSTEM

The canonical system of Figure 1 is a core configuration for *any* system that needs to perform smoothly, reliably, consistently, accurately… and, in short, a system that provides an acceptable performance in response to all the requirements [including events/disturbances external to this core system] over a timeline.

The dynamics of this canonical construct are addressed in greater detail in Appendix A. Basically, each of the entities of Figure 1 are processes that are not static but, in reality, vary with time. The function of Figure1 and its entities [sub-functions] can be viewed and used as organic in structure and behavior.

The poverty function in the canonical form of Figure 1 is provided in Figure 2; consider that the sub-functions, i.e., [1] – [7], must perform as an 'orchestra'. Now consider the outcome[s] if the same sub-functions simply do not perform together in a positive, acceptable and synergistic manner; what will that 'orchestra' sound like? This exercise is left to the readers' imaginations!

In similar fashion, Figure 3 provides the educational function in canonical form. Again, the systems of Figures 2 and 3 are not static over time but rather are dynamic systems in that the sub-functions of [1] - [7] vary in time and are a direct reflection of specific poverty site and educational arena dynamics.

Figure 4 offers the poverty function in canonical form and is expanded with its linkages to six clusters each of which contain a set of functions/sub-functions: {Prime Movers}, {Education}, {Performance}. {Legal & Justice Systems}, {Income & Employment} and {Requirements-Authority-Responsibility-Accountability}. **The Inequality Spectrum depicted in Figures 2, 3, 4 and 5 demonstrates the multidimensionality of poverty-driven 'systems', e.g., those within the inner cities and other poverty areas of America.**

The expansion process of the poverty system of Figure 4, including definitions and additional detail of each of the functions in the six clusters can be found at *Poverty-Inequalities.com*. This expansion process also applies to the education system [including its clusters of Figure 5} and can also be found at *Poverty-Inequalities.com*.

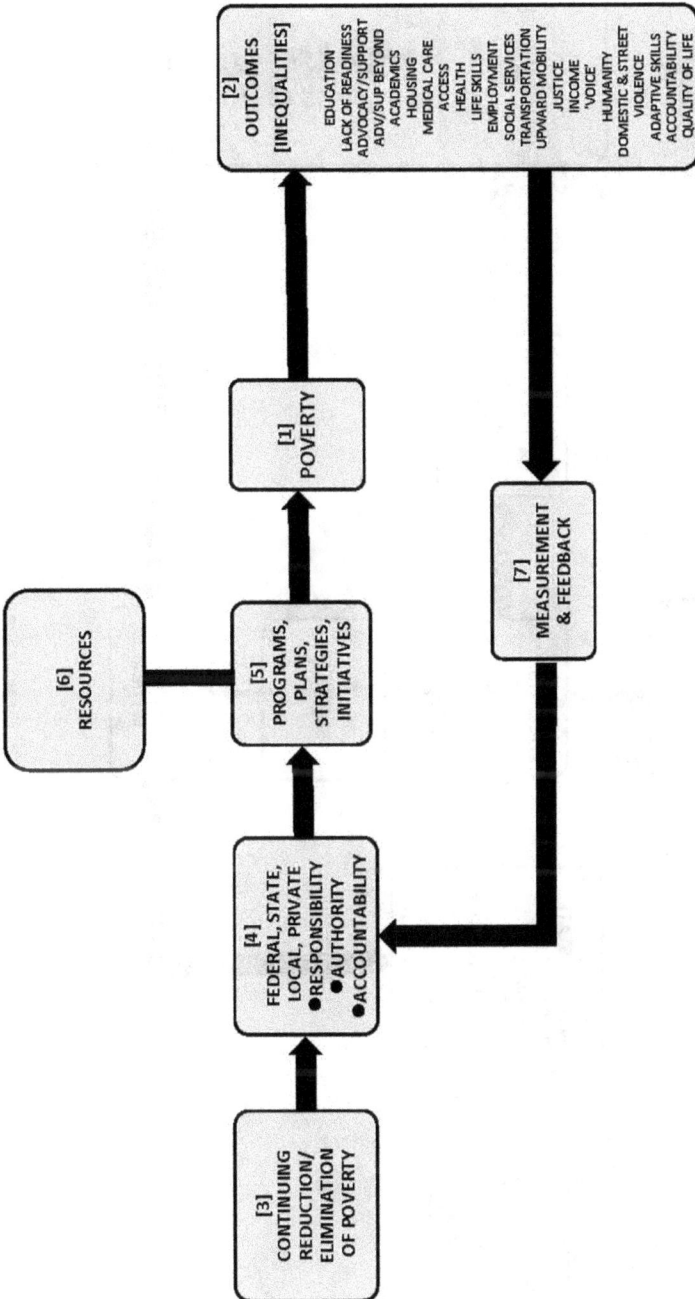

FIGURE 2 - POVERTY FUNCTION IN CANONICAL FORM

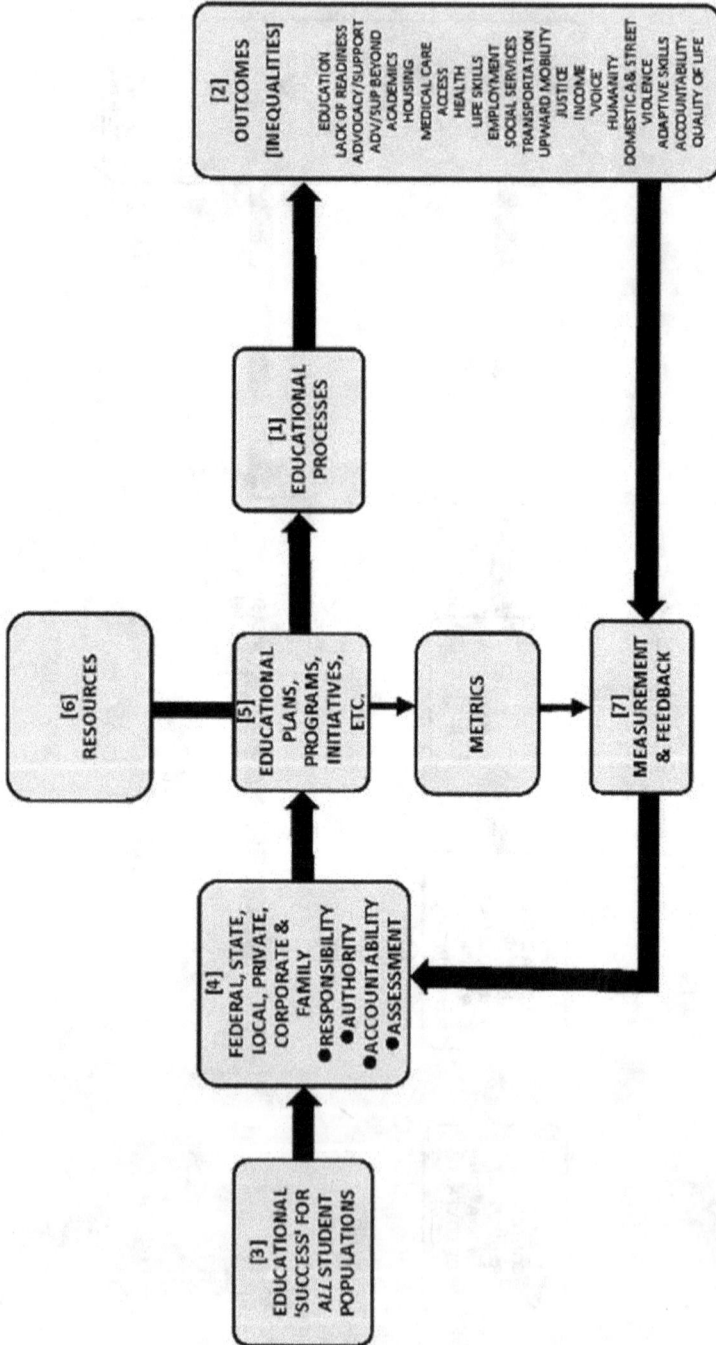

FIGURE 3 - EDUCATIONAL FUNCTION IN CANONICAL FORM

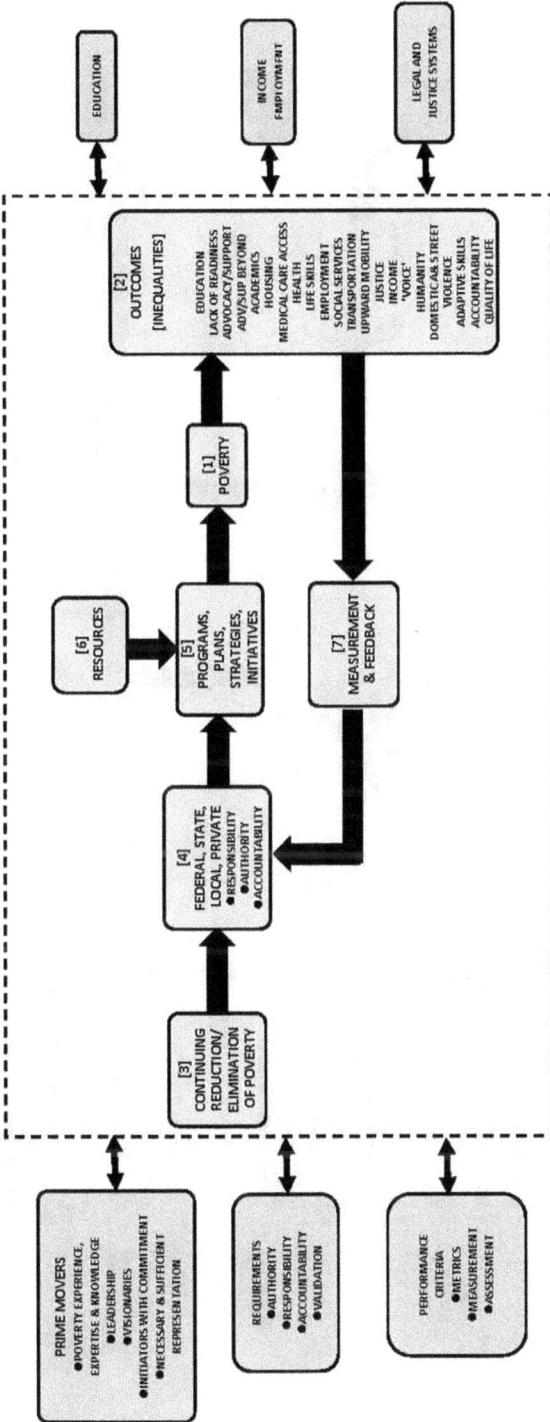

FIGURE 4 - POVERTY FUNCTION IN CANONICAL FORM WITH LINKAGES TO 'CLUSTER SETS.'

Colella & Crowley

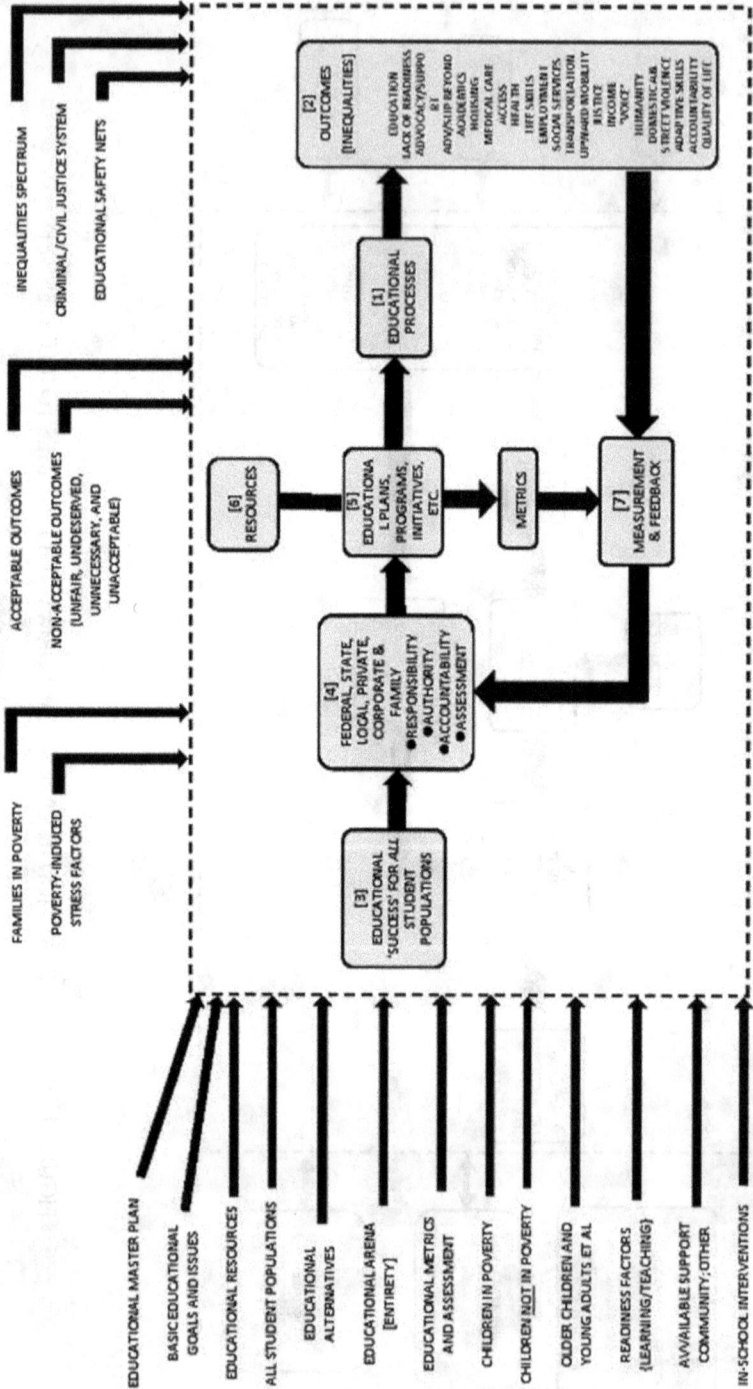

FIGURE 5 - EDUCATIONAL FUNCTION IN CANONICAL FORM WITH LINKAGES TO 'CLUSTER SETS.'

This website -- developed by the Innovative Group [Graphic Design & Digital Media] at the School of Engineering & Design at Johnson & Wales University -- provides a very user-friendly useful tool. The website attributes for both the poverty and educational functions and their respective 'linkages' and 'cluster sets' are addressed in Sections VI and VII, respectively. Users are able to use the website for a more detailed analysis of s situation/scenario shaped by the interests of the individual users.

EDUCATION and its LINKAGES

More to the point, this particular section could have been entitled 'The Poverty/Education Connection'. In the world of reality, 'the quality of Education' and 'poverty-enabled inequalities' are uniquely connected.

The odds of being poor are greatly increased if you are a child born into poverty. The road out of poverty is a good education. The greatest roadblock to a good education is to be born into poverty.

"Poor', being of low socio-economic status [SES], is a complex condition. There are urban, suburban and rural poor all manifesting their poverty in slightly different ways. There is situational poverty which may occur through a job loss, illness, divorce or other similar setbacks of life -- especially difficult for those living in poverty or marginally so. There is generational poverty in which poverty becomes a way of life, an organic culture, in which individuals and families learn survival by working the system of governmental, private support programs and even families. Yet, as diverse as poverty is, it produces strikingly similar symptoms one of which is a negative impact on a child's ability to learn.

Regardless of the type of poverty, living in poverty creates stresses in number, intensity, frequency and duration not typical in middle or upper class families [although middle class families transitioning to marginal and beyond are increasing: [R67], [R71]. Brain

41

damage is a consequence of children being exposed to too many stresses for durations. The chart to follow lists almost two dozen stress inducers. Children born into poverty begin life with the same potential as other children [unless the former has experienced improper prenatal care which may have interfered with their brain development]; it is the environment they live in which interferes with their ability to learn, to behave appropriately and to be as successful as children not plagued by the stresses of poverty.

Why this is so is well documented through hundreds of research studies. Research points to two intertwined conditions. Living in poverty provides little of the supports for education found in non-poverty homes -- the educationally impoverished home environment is a debilitating arena. And, the stresses of living in poverty interfere with brain development in ways critical to learning: {R63], [R64], [R65] and [R66].

STRESSORS
Inadequate nutrition
Food uncertainty
Housing instability
Poor quality of life
Single parenthood
Health Issues
Broken homes
Inadequate income
Inadequate education
Legal inequality
Justice inequality
Mainstream separation
Unproductive choices
Incarceration
Recidivism
Devalued education
Domestic violence/abuse
Street violence
Drug/alcohol use
Little upward mobility
Gang affiliations
Non-English speaking
Discrimination
Depression
Child care

Addressed here is the significant role education can play in preparing children for productive lives while also emphasizing that the schools cannot, by themselves and with their current [limited] resources, undo all of the impediments to learning triggered by growing up in poverty.

Suggested here is a reasoned approach to addressing poverty issues related to education so as to produce results not only improving student outcomes but, in fact, reducing the steadily rising social costs associated with risky behaviors that lead to teen pregnancy, drug and alcohol use, poor health and gang violence [R68]. Also mitigated would be the huge costs associated with incarceration and recidivism.

There are as many arguments, pro and con, as to why people are in poverty as there are arguments over what government interventions should be applied to assist those in poverty. There is one point upon which there is little argument. America would be a better place if it was understood our children are a national resource to be developed rather than squandered as we are currently doing.

A child in poverty scenario

Picture an inner city family living on the income of a single mother working a full time job and a part time job both for minimum wage. This is the life environment of the children.

The home generally provides little in terms of enrichment. There are few or no books or periodicals; if there is a computer, it is likely without internet service. Unlike in middle class homes, there are few, if any, after school classes in dance, art, music, karate nor Little League or similar athletic activities.

Conversations with adults provide about a third of the total words heard in a middle class home with far less variety and considerably more negative terms. One study suggests a three year old in a single parent family hears thirty million fewer words than does the child of parents who are professionals. Words are the tools used to learn, communicate, assimilate, and differentiate.

Unlike in middle class homes, medical and dental issues are likely to be untreated prior to becoming emergencies. The child may be sent to school sick since school is the child's daycare while the parent works.

Many parents, particularly those who were raised in poverty conditions, lack basic parenting skills. As such, they are more prone to what are referred to as 'harsh parenting' techniques: yelling, being physically domineering and using negative reinforcement rather than the positive reinforcement usually found in non-poverty homes.

The parents, more so those in generational poverty, value education less than middle class adults and impart this, both subliminally and otherwise, to their children. This has a two-prong impact. The children do not see education as valuable and the parents are less likely to work with the school to improve their children's educational outcomes and, by extension, the opportunity to learn some necessary life skills.

Our child's day in school begins the night before. **Playing outside is not particularly safe so the child watched television. There was no one available to help with the previous day's homework.** The eight year old goes to bed -- possibly with supper, possibly not. In the streets outside, there are cars driving by throughout the night with people yelling to the drug dealer next door. There are occasional gunshots heard throughout the neighborhood and the child has recently witnessed a gunshot victim. The mother's new boyfriend is in the house and the child is afraid of the new stranger. The child's body has activated the 'fight or flee' chemicals because the child is scared. But the child can neither fight nor flee.

The child's walk to school is littered with broken beer bottles, an assortment of discarded trash, drug paraphernalia and threatening gang members. The child may have a toothache but medical and dental issues are not a priority since mother has neither the time nor the resources to address them.

The child arrives at school. There is free breakfast -- which is good since there was no breakfast at home. The child walks into class. He or she has already been identified as a problem by the teacher since he or she arrives dirty with ill-fitting clothes. He/she has a problem sitting still and paying attention [direct results of the stresses to which the child is continuously exposed]. Then there is the toothache. The usual response of the teacher is to send the child to the principal or nurse to minimize disruption of the class -- a common form of classroom management. [Learning readiness, teaching readiness and classroom management are addressed in the forthcoming section]. The child has not done well on the prescribed standardized tests so must spend recess time and art class working on his/her literacy and math skills. The one bright spot in the child's day at school is lunch!

This is not an atypical scenario of inner city life for a child living in poverty. In some cases, conditions are not as bad, in other cases, far worse.

The role of education for children living in poverty

Various forces are in play relative to the education of children growing up in in a low socio-economic household. Unfortunately for the children, the forces tend to negatively impact their attempts at education.

Outcome of Stresses:
  [1] Impaired brain development
  [2] Inability to control behavior, limited short-term memory, and attention deficit disorder often lasting life-long.

Outcome of an environment of poverty. In comparison to more well-to-do children, a child in poverty has a smaller vocabulary, fewer literacy and math skills, suffers far more social and emotional issues, has less access to cultural enrichment and athletic activities, suffers from more malnutrition and untreated medical and dental conditions, and less access to reading materials and technology.

The two most negative forces coming into play are the **stresses of living in a poverty environment and the conditions the children** encounter that separate them from their more affluent and non-poverty peers and which create some of the oft referred to education 'gaps'.

Brain research has established the stress chemicals released as a result of multiple and long term stressors impair a child's ability to make sound behavioral judgments, create attention issues and impede short term memory; A perfect formula for school failure.

What happens to children coming to school with two such negatives: impaired brain development and a non-supportive home environment? Although they may represent a minority of school children, they represent the vast majority of students being retained, not achieving to the standards on assessments and not graduating.

The inspiration behind this observation is the one potentially bright light which, it is hoped, will illuminate the problem and lead to some solutions -- ***poverty is not destiny***. However, without interventions [and the 'readiness' factors to follow] it is extremely difficult for children to escape the world of poverty. The singular intervention offering the most promise can be aptly described as -- education is destiny with the caveat that education, must be effective since poor education is as much destiny as good education. A 'good education' process mandates that both the learning and teaching processes must be shaped to meet the needs of the students at hand.

There are those who will protest we have been spending billions of dollars educating children in poverty and supposedly empowering them for success and to what avail -- they still cannot pass the tests, pass from grade to grade, or graduate. The problem with this argument is that, yes, we have been offering education to these children. However, we are offering an education designed to meet the needs of middle and upper class children arriving at school from homes which complement and enhance the learning process. Poor children are ill equipped to succeed in a learning environment not at all suited to their needs. They are truly handicapped no less than the students being served by the Individuals with Disabilities Education Act [IDEA]. ***Stress has changed their brains and their home environments have not provided educational supports.***

Efforts to improve learning outcomes

Those outside of education, primarily legislatures, have attempted to address inadequate student outcomes by creating alternatives to our traditional public school system. Vouchers are designed to allow lower income parents to enroll their children in 'preferred' alternative private schools. Much of the research on vouchers would suggest they do little more than take money from the cash strapped public schools.

Charter schools present themselves quite differently. Charter schools have been created in myriad forms throughout the country purportedly to be incubators of innovation -- innovations that ostensibly would be models for the public schools to emulate. Most national research on charters suggest results across the country are little different from those in Chicago. The charter school initiative in Chicago is the primary reason Arne Duncan was the United States Secretary of Education. The latest information from Chicago [R70] indicates roughly one third of the charters are doing better than the public schools they replaced, one third are doing the same and one third are not doing as well. Current mayor, Rahm Emanuel, has been quoted as saying the charters are doing a 'little' better than the public schools before them.

There is no question some charter schools are doing superlative work -- including work with children in poverty. There are those who suggest creating more of these schools using the same model. Two reasons are offered as to why this is not the most prudent course. The first is the reality that there are charter schools, and a number of public schools, identified as being outstanding in what they accomplish with students in poverty who accomplish these results through herculean commitments from administrators and teachers. Cloning the methods used in such a school without cloning the staff commitment will not achieve the same outcomes. The second reason is the aforementioned 'incubator' rationale for the creation of charter schools. Where a methodology is found to be effective in a charter school, one would expect the same methodology could or should be introduced into public schools serving the same student demographics. Creating more of the same model charter is a recipe for failure. The charter school model is incapable of being brought to scale. Charter schools will never fully replace public schools. At this juncture, the charters are impacting public schools much the same way as vouchers. Limited fiscal resources are being directed to charters at the expense of the other public schools. Students who are lucky enough to gain entry to the successful charter schools are identified as the 'winners'. It is not difficult to figure out what that makes the students left behind. Nor to figure out the impression created of the public schools the children are leaving.

Then there is the argument the charters are open to every student since enrollment is most often based on a lottery system. As with any lottery, you have to have a ticket to have a chance. Parents most concerned about their children's education will enter those children in the lottery. Having involved parents is critical to student learning and many charters require very specific parental engagement. Children of parents who are not that involved with education for any vast number of reasons -- most poverty driven -- are not likely to ever enter a charter school. As a side note, since charters tend to attract involved parents away from other public schools, it is difficult to comprehend why the charters are not consistently outperforming the public schools.

Education as human resource development

A background note: following World War II, both Japan and Germany found themselves in dire straits. Both economies had been shattered, their male populations had been decimated, Germany's manufacturing capacity was destroyed, and both countries had large areas laid to waste. Interestingly, both countries, in beginning reconstruction, came to the same conclusion. Their primary natural resource, the foundation of future success, was their people. Germany and Japan needed to develop their human resources. And they did!

First world countries provide a stark contrast to third world countries. First world countries have literate and educated populations able to contribute to the national good. Third world countries have large populations of illiterate and uneducated who serve to drain the meager resources of these countries and contribute little.

America provides an interesting contrast. Although America has long been considered first world, we have large numbers of partially literate and poorly educated citizens. America's poor, those most likely to lack educations and the ability to contribute to society, constitute a significant percentage of the population. According to the National Center of Children in Poverty, 22% of our children live below the federal dollar defined poverty level and 45% are considered to be living in low-income families [R67, R71]. It should be an embarrassment that, of all the first world countries, America is tied with Romania for having the most children in poverty. [By the UNICEF definition of poverty, living below 60% of the national median income, The United States has a 31% child poverty rate.]

The number of children living in poverty has been growing [R74]. According to the National Center of Children in Poverty, in 2000 the number was 17%, in 2013 it had risen to 22%. Although this percentage did decrease several percent since then, the overall increasing trend remains quite significant. The increasing numbers of children in poverty correlates to decreases in the federal budget related to supports for children.

American student outcomes have been a source of dissatisfaction for decades. However, when one disaggregates test scores by demographics, many American students are doing as well as or better than their international peers. The one demographic whose student outcomes consistently fall below the standard, bringing down the national average, is students living in poverty.

Granted, other minority groups do suffer from discriminatory practices. In speaking to this issue, Robert Pasternak [R72], education consultant and former Assistant Secretary in the U.S. Department of Education, suggests upward of 75% of the learning gaps associated with racial minorities can be attributed to living in poverty. This would lead one to believe addressing the impact of poverty on education would result in improving the outcomes for all children in poverty and would reduce the [learning] gaps for racial minorities considerably.

We need to ask ourselves, why, in America, do we allow third world conditions which, as noted above, drain national resources rather than contribute? Forgetting the quality of life for those living in poverty would be much improved should they be able to work themselves out, would not everyone in the country benefit from having , as Mitch Romney in his presidential bid so eloquently stated, fewer 'takers' and more 'givers'? Would America's middle class not benefit greatly from not having to support those not currently able to adequately support themselves?

Human resources are developed through sound educational systems designed to provide all youth with the capacity to be productive, contributing citizens of the communities in which they reside. Sound educational systems recognize the needs of the community and tailor themselves to those needs while in concert with the needs of the individual.

Given the needs of diverse student populations across America, does the 'one size doesn't fit all' strategy make any sense -- educationally? Ignoring the needs of either the individual or community results in wasteful mix matches of human resources. [A system suggesting four year college degrees for everyone, thus focusing on the individual, totally ignores the realities of the community in which seventy percent of occupations, some of whose monetary rewards may equal or better the jobs of college graduates].

Finland, Canada and Australia provide an interesting contrast to the United States. The three countries' educational outcomes far exceed, on average, those of the United States. The qualifier, 'on average', is noted because America's student outcomes, should one remove the low socio-economic status children, would move considerably up the outcome scale. It is not that the country is doing such a poor job of educating middle and upper class children, it is because the country does such a dismal job of educating its children living in poverty and having such large numbers of children in poverty that it compares so poorly to other countries. And, it should be noted, the countries with the superlative student outcomes are not without children in poverty. Learning gaps exist in each country between socio-economic strata. But, by comparison, Finland reports only 5% of its children as living in poverty -- with much smaller learning gaps.

Finland, Canada and Australia all provide safety nets for children. The countries exhibit a 'family consciousness' not found in America. America's attitude, all too frequently, is the poor are poor due to their own shortcomings and, if they would only pull themselves up, would not be poor. Assistance is given begrudgingly and reduced at every opportunity.

A Canadian study found national investments in assisting low SES children to achieve academically provided a nine per cent annual return on investment -- by age 30 a child thus supported had paid back, through paying more taxes and requiring fewer services, all of the costs for extra support. And this benefit continues through his or her life. This particular relationship between poverty, education, up-front [early] investments into the educational processes and a remarkable return-on-investment [ROI] is addressed in greater detail both in forthcoming sections of this book and at Poverty-Inequalities.com.

As the Finnish education expert, Paul Sahlberg [R73], has stated on a number of occasions, Finland's education outcomes are superlative due in part to a significant difference between that country's education objectives and America's and just how those outcomes are achieved. As he sees it, America educates to maximize the earning power of graduates. Finland educates to minimize the societal costs of its graduates -- welfare, health, incarceration, etc. Finland provides a number of supports for its youth which lead to better student outcomes.

According to the 2009 Kinsey report, The Economic Impact of the Achievement Gap in America's School [R75], if American schools had performed to the same level as Finnish schools, the American

GDP would have been $1.3 to $1.4 trillion higher. Surely, a staggering number by itself but when paired with hundreds of billions of dollars America spends on welfare, food stamps, unemployment, medical services related to poverty, and incarceration, one begins to visualize the true cost of not investing in our children. America does not provide the support early on but suffers the consequences later.

Not investing in the education of children, our most important natural resource, is not only shortsighted, it actually perpetuates and potentially increases those taxes contributed by the general population and consumes a lot of tax supported resources.

As a consequence of the negative school experience, children passing into adulthood, experience higher unemployment, greater health issues, higher instances of single parenthood and, among other things, considerably higher incarceration rates. Thus, the societal costs of not properly educating this group of students are significant.

A guide published by the National Association of Elementary School Principals, **Leading Pre-K-3 Learning Communities**, addresses the potential payback of investments in providing additional supports for children living in poverty. A mere $20 invested in early childhood education produces savings of $9.63 in education, $18.57 in additional taxes and $3.65 in welfare savings. That alone is over a 150% return. However, there is an astounding $226 in crime and punishment savings. [In the subsequent section on poverty and brain development, there is discussion on how the brain's executive function, which controls behavior, is adversely impacted by the stresses of living in poverty and how this may relate to criminal activity.]

According to the 2009 Kinsey study, [R75], which reported that our Gross Disposable Product would have increased by $400-$670 **billion** had the gap between low SES students and higher SES students been narrowed. *That is an annual payback!* Poverty not only harms the impoverished, it harms us all.

The educationally impoverished home environment

Children born into poverty begin with the same potential as other children; it is the environment in which they live which interferes with their ability to learn., to behave appropriately and to be as successful as children not plagued by the stresses of poverty,

John Hattie [R76], an internationally recognized education researcher in his *Visible Learning - A Synthesis of over 800 meta-analyses relating to achievement [2009],* reports on various conditions impacting education outcomes. Over seven and a half million students were involved as subjects in various studies. In his work, Hattie sorted the mega analyses [research studies analyzing the findings of multiple other studies of a topic to glean insights into the following findings which are consistent across all of the other studies] into twenty one categories.

The following are some of the findings as they relate to living in poverty. Prior achievement is highly correlated to current and future achievement. The child in poverty who has fallen behind is highly likely to stay behind.

Self concept has a medium influence on student outcomes. Children in poverty, particularly those in schools with more affluent classmates, recognize the difference between themselves and others. Even clothing, something many would consider inconsequential, is a stressor for impoverished children.

Motivation falls in the medium influence range. A child living in poverty is frequently the child of someone not well educated. The impact of parental attitudes towards school and education is likely to be negative resulting in the child not seeing school as important. Juxtapose a parent with little education and ill equipped to support a child's school efforts with a middle class parent supporting and 'pushing' a child. Which child is likely to be motivated to learn?

Ruby Payne, [R26], [R27], education author and consultant, lists how the lower, middle and upper classes relate to topics such as food, money, friends, work and education. A child living in a home with generational poverty is unlikely to perceive education as a means of escape from the poverty conditions. That attitude plus the combined effects of poverty stressors and other impediments to learning often lead to other routes of escape, e.g., gang membership or participation in the drug dealing arena.

Another medium influence on student outcomes is 'concentration, persistence and engagement'. As will be addressed later, a child living with the stresses associated with poverty is undergoing brain changes that seriously inhibit all three -- concentration, persistence and engagement. In addition, children are often disciplined for not exhibiting one of the three which further serves to exacerbate the difficulties of the educational process. A related issue, addressed by Hattie, is anxiety -- a medium influencer. Although he reserves his findings to primarily test and math anxiety, an impoverished child has far more to be anxious about -- the effects of which are reported below.

Birth weight, specifically, low birth weight, is a serious problem for mothers who often do not have proper prenatal care, proper nutrition, and are more likely to smoke or drink during pregnancy. Birth weight is a medium influence on student outcomes. Pre-mature birth, a condition arising much more often to low SES mothers due to the lack of prenatal care, is another indicator of future learning problems which translates to a lack of 'learning readiness' as addressed in the forthcoming section. According to *Time* magazine, when it comes to premature births, America ranks with Somalia, Turkey and Thailand with twelve of one hundred births. Belarus has five of a hundred.

On the positive side of Hattie's study is that both early intervention and preschool programs have positive impacts on student outcomes. As will be noted, leveling the playing field for children living in poverty must be started long before conventional schooling. The 'learning gaps' do not occur as a child reached his or her fifth birthday. They are developing from the time the conditions that create a low birth weight began.

Hattie's research, when one adds all of the high and medium influencing conditions as they relate to poverty, would suggest the 'deck' is stacked against the child living in poverty. His findings led him to this statement: "The home can be a nurturing place for the achievement of students, or it can be a toxic mix of harm and neglect with respect to enhancing learning." He concedes that many parents start out with positive expectations for their children. Of course, it is where the child ends up that counts.

A reading of Hattie would suggest living in poverty harms learning outcomes and the impact of neglect, where it occurs, compounds the problem.

Although not directly bringing it into his research, Hattie does comment on the communication skills development of impoverished children. His report suggests that by school age, needy children hear 4,500,000 words while wealthier children hear 6,500,000. There are other researchers who suggest the ratio is closer to one to five -- 600 versus 3000 words per day. Hart and Risley, of the University of Kansas, concluded there was a 30,000,000 word difference between those heard by the children of two professionals versus those in a welfare home - by age three. Not only do these children hear fewer words but the vocabulary used is much less broad and the ratio of positive to negative words is almost totally reversed. Words are the tools used to learn, to frame ideas, to assess, to differentiate, to think, to express one self. Research suggests the tool boxes of impoverished children are far smaller than those of their peers such that their ability to learn, assess, think and express is seriously impeded.

The surface has only been scratched as to the differences of living in poverty versus being raised in a middle or upper class home. The impoverished home generally provides little in terms of enrichment -- it provides far less educationally-related stimulation. There are few or no books or periodicals, if there is a computer it is likely without internet service/access. There are few toys. Unlike middle class homes, there are no after school classes in dance, art, music, karate nor Little League or similar athletic activities. There are no vaca-tions, visits to museums, libraries, trips to zoos and aquariums. Unlike in middle class homes, medical and dental issues are unlikely to be treated unless they are emergencies. The best teacher in the world is not going to be able to teach over a toothache.

Many parents raised in poverty conditions lack basic parenting skills. As such, they are more prone to what are referred to as 'harsh parenting' techniques -- yelling, being physically domineering, using corporal punishment and using negative reinforcement rather than the positive and constructive reinforcement usually found in affluent homes. Children in poverty are much more often the victims of phys-ical, sexual and emotional abuse.

Needy children often have parents working very hard to pay the rent and buy the food. Parents, particularly single parents who make up a large percentage of poverty households, may work multiple lobs at minimum wages. The work schedule provides little time or en-ergy to support a child's learning. The child may be watching fifty or sixty hours of television per week; Hattie suggests anything over ten hours is detrimental to the child. Sleep is unregulated. Food may be fast food due to the lack of time to shop and cook... leading to some cases to the strange combination of malnutrition and obesity. All of the stresses impact the parent as much as, or more than, the child which leads to a negative impact on the relationship between child and par-ent.

The home may lack appropriate space for learning activities such as homework. Due to parent work schedules older children may be responsible for younger children -- a circumstance frequently lead-ing to absenteeism of the older child if day care is not available or affordable. Absenteeism is itself more prevalent for needy children due to more illnesses, lack of appropriate clothing, parental negligence or apathy, transportation and other issues. Amongst other issues, there is a growing suspicion -- and some documented evidence that the sui-cide rate for children in poverty has been steadily increasing for sev-eral decades.

A condition covered more thoroughly in the coming paragraphs is the lack of nurturing in a low SES household. As noted, the parents are equally as stressed as the children. Work, worry about money, the same exposure to the negatives of living in a poverty environment as their children plus the worry about their children consumes the time and energy of parents living in poverty such that there is little of the parent left to interact with their children in positive ways. Nurturing activities -- kind, supportive, comforting interaction between parent and child -- are often minimal at best or totally lacking at worst. In generational poverty, many non-nurturing parents are children of non-nurturing parents which not only perpetuates a problem but the non-nurturing parents of several children simply multiplies the problem.

[The classic case in point relative to nurturing is the Communist bloc orphanages employing 'warehousing' techniques which tended to the physical needs of infants but provided little or no nurturing. Brain development in these infants was half of normal and many simply died.]

As alluded to in the introduction, living in poverty provides myriad incentives to move out of poverty. Poverty is not a nice place to live for the child or the parent. The road out of poverty goes directly through the schoolhouse. Unfortunately for the children, the foregoing is a list of the roadblocks impeding their chance/opportunity to successfully travel through school and escape poverty -- for them and, tragically for *their* children.

The notion of 'failing' schools

Johns Hopkins University presents an interesting contradiction. For many years, the University published its Dropout Factory list -- a list of high schools with exceptionally high dropout rates. Invariably, the schools served inner city, high poverty populations. Coincidentally [should you believe in coincidences], the University was doing research in the Baltimore public schools. The Baltimore findings suggested children living in poverty were, through the lower grades, falling behind year by year. However, when learning was analyzed between September and June, the children in poverty were learning as essentially the same rate as the more affluent students. Children in poverty fell behind between June and September when the middle class students enjoyed the privileges of being middle class, On the one hand, Johns Hopkins was blasting high schools for failing children in poverty and, on the other hand, claiming the gaps that led to dropout rates were not the fault of the schools.

Then, along came the federal government. The current national education policies blame the schools for less than optimal learning by children living in poverty. The assumption being schools can fix what poverty has created. They cannot. Schools cannot fix poverty. Low student achievement is a symptom of poverty. As noted around the world, student outcomes will be related to the extent of poverty of which the students are victims. Student outcomes improve when poverty is meaningful addressed. Substandard student outcomes, the learning gaps, are a symptom of a problem. Yet, our government programs have led the public to believe learning gaps are the problem. This, in turn, has led to 'remedies' which have not diminished the learning gaps. One cannot 'fix' symptoms and expect the problem which created the symptoms will disappear. Poverty, per se, is the problem which creates unsatisfactory learning outcomes for children living in poverty. Firing teachers and closing schools will not 'cure' poverty.

No Child Left behind [NCLB], America's first federal government education initiative, is a noble thought. However, in execution, NCLB has perpetrated a cruel hoax on America's poor. NCLB suggested all children were to be able to achieve to a certain educational level regardless of socio-economic status or a number of other factors usually associated with lower education achievement. Parents were encouraged, when their child did not achieve to the same level as middle class children to seek alternative schools. Alternative schools were to replace the 'underperforming' public schools. As noted earlier, no country in the world has totally eliminated differences in student outcomes based on socio-economics. While our public schools are being seriously harmed by the 'alternative' schools, the alternative schools have been achieving, on average, the same results as the schools they replaced. NCLB is essentially a federal program designed to shift the blame for poverty impaired learning outcomes from the federal program that should be addressing childhood poverty to the schools which do not have the resources to treat the symptoms poverty creates. In the meantime, public schools are constantly disparaged at their inability to do what the federal government should be doing.

In essence, the federal government created a system of standardized testing with achievement levels to be attained by all students without assuring all students would be receiving the same resources in preparing for the tests -- children in poverty do not bring to the tests all of the supports more affluent children bring from home. The federal government then blamed schools for the results -- labeling the schools 'failing'. The federal government laid the groundwork that assured schools serving large populations of children in poverty would fall short of the federal mandates. In this way, the federal government created 'failing' schools. The federal government then used 'failing' schools to promote its agenda of 'alternative' schools and attacks on the educators working in the supposedly 'failing' schools. To many observers, No Child Left behind was an insidious attack on public schools.

Poverty, stress and brain development

"One of the things that is important here is that the infants' brains look very similar at birth." This is a quote from Seth Poliak of the University of Wisconsin - Madison and as reported in Science Daily. However, brain development quickly begins to differ between needy and more affluent children. Brain volumes by age three can differ by over 15% according to the UWM researchers.

The question arises: "Why should a brain develop less in needy children? Considerable research points to stresses and the body's response to stress. Stress is, as it was designed to be, a good thing. It prepares the body for 'fight' or 'flight' life saving responses. But, what if one can neither fight nor flee as in the case of a young child living in poverty?

In that case, the brain is exposed to a constant bath of cortisol -- the chemical produced by the body to prepare muscles and brain for immediate action. Living in poverty is highly stressful. There are food and housing uncertainty, violence in the house and on the streets, struggles in school. There are worries about money and safety. Whereas some cortisol is beneficial, a steady flow of unabated cortisol is toxic.

Paul Tough, in *How Children Succeed*, [R78], reports on research accomplished by Michael Meany of McGill University [Canada]. Meany's researchers were performing experiments with baby rats and noticed the rats were stressed by their handling. Upon being returned to their cages, some mothers performed a nurturing 'licking and grooming' procedure on the stressed babies which led to a reduction in stress related behaviors. Other babies, whose mothers were not nurturing, continued to be stressed.

Curiosities piqued, the researchers turned to recording the characteristics of each group of rats as they matured. They reported the nurtured learned more, were more social, more curious, less aggressive, exhibited more self control, were healthier and lived longer.

Meady's research was on baby rats. What about baby people? The Adverse Childhood Experiences research by Vincent Felitti and Robert Anda of the Kaiser Permanente, a California HMO, also reported in [R77], measured the childhood stresses reported by 17,000 adults and then took an inventory. Those with the most stresses were more obese, suffered more depression, had earlier sexual experiences, higher incidents of smoking, drug use and alcoholism and suffered more cancer, heart disease, liver disease and COPD.

Professor of Psychiatry, Joan Luby, at the Washington School of Medicine in St. Louis published the results of a study on 145 children in JAMA Pediatrics [R79]. Luby's report mirrors the work done at McGill University. Essentially, her findings concluded stresses release cortisol which leads to brain changes which result in hyperactivity and attention deficits. The JAMA Pediatrics abstract states "Findings substantiate the behavioral literature on negative effects of poverty on child development and provide new data confirming that effects extend to brain development.

Teaching with Poverty in Mind [2009] by Eric Jensen reports on the importance of 'unconditional love, guidance and support' during the first three years of a child's life. It is during this time that such bonding "helps them develop a wider range of healthy emotions, including gratitude, forgiveness and empathy. He goes on to say: "Deficits in these areas inhibit the production of new brain cells, alter the path of maturation and rework the healthy neural circuitry in children's brains, thereby undermining emotional and social development and predisposing them to emotional dysfunction."

The stresses of growing up in a poverty environment are well documented. Food uncertainty, housing uncertainty, violence in the home and on the neighborhood, untreated health issues, harsh parenting practices, drug and alcohol use in the home, higher levels of physical, emotional and sexual abuse have a cumulative impact. Often children will be at home alone while both parents or a single parent works multiple low-paying jobs.

The antidote to these destructive stress forces, according to the research, is the influence of a warm and caring adult. Unfortunately, many children living in poverty do not have in their homes an adult capable of providing the needed warmth and care. In the McGill University study mentioned above, researchers found parents who were themselves deprived of a warm and caring environment as children, were often incapable of providing the same for their children.

How do brain changes and being raised in poverty stricken households manifest themselves in school? Jensen lists 'acting out behaviors: impatience, and impulsivity, gaps in politeness and social graces, more limited range of behavioral responses and less empathy for other's misfortunes. None of the above are likely to engender positive responses from teachers or peers.

Taking into consideration the brain development issues related to the stresses of living in poverty, there is little wonder such children are more often involved in disciplinary procedures in school and, then, in the juvenile and criminal justice systems. If one's brain has been impaired by stress induced chemicals which cause hyperactivity and short attention spans, how could these children *not* get into trouble? The usual disciplinary model of 'progressive discipline' moves a child from one level of discipline to another with suspension or expulsion being the ultimate penalties. The resultant absenteeism only exacerbates the already high levels of absenteeism of these children.

And that is merely the social interaction of learning. Other brain changes are even more central to the learning process. The over production of cortisol has been found to not only inhibit brain growth in children but to cause the atrophy of the amygdala and hippocampus. Since these brain parts are crucial to behavior, which is controlled by the brain's executive function, and short term memory, it is little wonder how SES children could have 'learning gaps'. If little Johnny lacks the understanding and the control to sit quietly and he is unable to retain what is being taught, we have the answer to "Why can't Johnny read?"

The most effective antidote to extreme, constant stresses is nurturing -- be it in the home, school, day care center, Boys or Girls Club or Scout den.

Moving children out of poverty

   As noted in the opening paragraph, 'The greatest opportunity one has to rise from poverty is through education.' All of the financial benefits to the nation noted above resulting from reducing the number of citizens in poverty is based on the cumulative benefits to the individual moving out of poverty. Parents are able to provide food, housing and medical care for their children in a home without the stresses of street crime, fiscal uncertainty and unresolved drug and alcohol issues are parents who are themselves less stressed. Moving children living in poverty to a middle class environment, with all of the advantages that status conveys, will afford those children the opportunity to achieve academically and socially at the same pace as middle class children. That is the goal and the potential provided by a meaningful education. Achieving that goal, even to the point our children living in poverty were to be reduced to the levels in a country like Finland, is a long term effort. There are no quick solutions.

   In the meantime, our schools will attempt to address the symptoms associated with living in property. But the schools need help. Schools need children not damaged by the lack of prenatal care. Schools need children who have been nurtured through their early years -- through programs supporting parents in child rearing skills and in providing surrogates in the form of early childhood caregivers. Schools need children who have been properly nourished and who have been afforded appropriate pediatric medical and dental care. Schools need children who are living in stable housing -- not needing to move when the rent is due and no money is available. And, as simple as it is, schools need children who have winter coats and boots that allow the child to attend school regardless of the weather.

   And the schools? The schools need to have the resources to expand their reach. A child living in poverty needs resources not found in the home of the poor, pre-schools, from the earliest ages, can provide toys and play opportunities, e.g. [R18], ; communication skill development, socialization skills and access to zoos, children's museums, dance and music instruction. "What the best and wisest parents wants their own children, that must be the community want for all of its children.' Some of the wisdom of John Dewey, one of America's foremost education thinkers. We cannot wait until a child reaches five years old to provide what the best and wisest parent wants for her or his child. By then significant gaps in learning have been created between our have and have-not children. It is essential to not allow these gaps to form in the first place.

And once in school? The one program offered to a portion of our needy children is Head Start. It is a preschool program designed to close the learning gaps of children in poverty prior to their entering kindergarten. It provides many of the supports noted previously. But Head Start has been disparaged since the gaps closed by the program reappear by the third grade. One has to wonder why anyone would think this would be different. Learning gaps are a symptom of poverty. If the poverty has not been 'cured', the symptom will continue to be exhibited. Anyone with a cold taking cough medicine knows that if the medicine is stopped before the cold is cured the cough will reappear. Learning gap/poverty and cough/cold. The symptoms will persist until the underlying cause is corrected. The supports to children living in poverty, as noted below, must be provided until the child is no longer in poverty -- for optimal results, right through college and other arenas of education.

America does support its children living in poverty in one long standing program. But, America being America, it should probably be noted the program providing free and reduced price lunches for children meeting certain poverty guidelines was not motivated so much to alleviate the nutrition problems of needy children as it was to support farm prices for the agriculture industry. Earlier on, the program provided tons and tons of surplus farm commodities purchased by the federal government to be used for free lunches [this was done to maintain farm prices]. However, the program, which now includes free breakfasts, provides some of the absolute best evidence that intervening to offset the problems of growing up in poverty is effective. The damage to children, of which their educations would only play a small part, of taking away these two meals provided on school days would be catastrophic. Not only for the children but for their families who often depend on the food their school children receive in school to spread their meager food resources to other family members.

Simply put, schools need to level the playing field between needy and more well-to-do students. What middle class children receive as a birthright all children need. As noted, 'school' must be offered to children from an early age. Middle class parents read to and communicate with their children. Schools must work with low SES parents to do the same and to complement and supplement the process as needed.

Schools need, through extended day and school year programs, to provide the enrichment that middle class children benefit from in dance, music, art classes; from participation in Little League and other athletic pursuits; from visits to local museums, libraries, zoos and theaters. Even taking a child from a concrete neighborhood to a park to simply run around in a safe environment, e.g., [R2].

Within the school day, a child living in poverty needs additional supports. The homework easily accomplished in a middle class home may be impossible in a poverty ridden home -- frequently overcrowded, lacking space with no distractions, and lacking the types of parental supports provided by middle class parents. A meaningful and consistent after-school homework program would go a long way in supporting the day school program but would also provide extended day care for parents needing that help.

Schools, because they are the one place children can be relied upon to attend, need to coordinate clinics providing medical and dental interventions -- including hearing and eye tests. *Time* [September, 2015], Alexandra Sifferlin's article, How to make school better for kids, provides eight recommendations one of which is to screen kids for mental illness. This particular recommendation could very well be a pre-emptive component within a comprehensive health program, i.e., medical, dental, hearing, sight and educationally related psychological issues. Schools can be the vehicle through which child wellcare services can be provided to minimize the damage caused by the lack of health care and undiagnosed conditions -- particularly conditions such as diabetes and obesity. Aligned with this would be schools working with parents to assure proper nutrition including working with local agencies to assure healthy food choices being available to families in need.

And, once again, the schools working with children and their families need to provide the nurturing that, because developing brains are so malleable, offsets the damage of stress induced cortisol.

Each of the interventions suggested above have been researched. A simple Google search will provide from a few to myriad projects noting the relationship between interventions for needy children and learning outcomes. One can draw additional conclusions by investigating the supports for children in poverty provided by countries with far better learning outcomes that America experiences -- countries which may not have eliminated the learning gaps associated with socio-economics but have reduced them considerably from those experienced in the United States.

Behavior and crime

Just as student outcomes are lower in poverty stricken neighborhoods, crime is higher. Gang violence is virtually exclusive to areas of poverty. Is there more than a casual relationship between student outcomes and crime?

As noted above, excessive cortisol, the product of extreme and unabated stresses associated with living in poverty, interferes with the brain's executive function. The brain's executive function controls behavior. Damage to the amygdala and hippocampus inhibit a child's ability to differentiate between right and wrong. In school, lack of behavioral control leads to aggression, inappropriate responses and what are considered to be 'acting out' activities.

Another characteristic of a child raised by a parent who does not know how or who has too little time to appropriately nurture the child is a lack of empathy. The child does not understand and cannot feel the emotions of others.

Why would a young man randomly shoot into a group of people over some real or imagined slight? Why would anyone sell drugs to someone who is obviously being destroyed by the drugs? Why would someone hook a young girl on drugs so as to prostitute her? These are not normal, acceptable behaviors. These are examples of individuals unable to relate to the victims of the crimes they are committing.

Empathy is the foundation of pro-social activities. Conversely, a lack of empathy explains antisocial behaviors. One would have to believe any efforts to support the development of empathy would ultimately lead to less crime overall.

In one study previously mentioned, something as simple as a pre-school intervention produced an 1100% return-on-investment in crime and punishment savings. In a 2003 report, *The Effect of Education on Crime: Evidence from Prison Inmates, Arrests and Self-Reports*, by Lance Lochner, Department of Economics, University of Western Ontario and Enrico Moretti, Department of Economics, UCLA, the authors conclude: "The estimated social externalities from reduced crime are sizable [sic]. A 1% increase in the high school completion rate of all men ages 20-60 would save the United States as much as $1,4 billion per year in reduced costs from crime incurred by victims and society at large. Such externalities from education amount to $1,170-$2100 per additional high school graduate or 14-26% of the private return to schooling. It is difficult to imagine a better reason to develop policies that prevent high school drops [sic.]" As will be noted later, this research assumes causality between high school graduation and lower incarceration rates when, in fact, low graduation rates and high incarceration rates may come from the same cause -- poverty.

The connections between incarceration and poverty are well documented. The poor go to jail more often, stay longer and return more often than do the middle class. America, with its high rate of poverty, also has, according to Wikipedia, an incarceration rate astronomically higher than other English speaking countries. In America, 707 of every 100,000 people are incarcerated -- in England, 148; Australia, 143 and Canada, 118. In fact, from the same data, America has the second highest incarceration rate in the world. The costs for maintaining this system are staggering.

Studies by Keith McBurnett and others published by the University of Chicago [2000] and funded by the National Institutes of Health came to this conclusion: "Low salivary levels of the stress hormone cortisol are associated with early onset and persistence of aggressive behavior. Boys with consistently low levels began antisocial acts younger, exhibited three times as many symptoms of conduct disorder and were three times as likely to be named by their classmates as 'meanest'. The same indicator was found in young pregnant girls who also exhibited above average levels of depression.

McBurnett does not draw a conclusion as to why cortisol is related to aggression nor why certain children exhibit abnormal levels -- allowing it could be a result of birth or subsequent influences. McBurnett does not relate salivary cortisol to the production of total cortisol. However, subsequent research directly relates high cortisol levels to stresses and the stresses associated with living in poverty. The research also targets the damage caused by cortisol to the developing brain and the impact on behavior, short term memory and the ability to concentrate.

Conclusions

"The odds of being poor are greatly increased if you are a child born into poverty. The road out of poverty is a good education. The greatest roadblock to a good education is to be born into poverty." Generational poverty and the beginnings of generations of poverty are rooted in low educational achievement. In terms of cause and effect, the conditions surrounding a childhood in poverty, both the impoverished living conditions and the associated stresses, lead to educational outcomes less than those of children not born into poverty.

Assuring an appropriate education for children living in poverty needs to start at the same time their more affluent peers begin being primed for educational opportunities -- with prenatal care. Premature and low birth weights both correlate to later cognitive deficits. Providing the same intellectual stimulation and communication exposure throughout early childhood as higher SES children receive primes the lower SES students for schooling. Appropriate nurturing in both the home and school reduces the potential brain damage associated with the over-production of cortisol.

The adverse impact of living in poverty does not abate simply because a child is in school. Middle and upper class children are provided myriad activities which enhance, support, complement and supplement their school experiences. A Wallace Foundation research study in 2004 suggested that 40% of these variables associated with student learning were attributable to influences "outside of the school." Children in poverty need the same activities through early pre-school supports and throughout their schooling -- as long as the poverty conditions exist. It will be shown in the forthcoming section that 'learning readiness' must be addressed through all educational processes -- conventional or otherwise.

Schools are a primary source of supports for children in poverty. However, poverty is a social issue and thus needs a variety of social supports. Childcare, counseling, medical and dental care, activities for children, parental supports, stable housing and adequate nutrition are issues other entities than schools can address. The role of government in addressing issues of poverty has been dismal in America since the demise of the Great Society programs of the 1970s. That was the period that witnessed an actual decrease in the learning gaps between poor and non-poverty students. Since that time, the number of children living in poverty has increased to the point that more than one in five children are designated as living in poverty. The metric used for this designation was income dollars; of course, as previously noted, poverty is multidimensional and there is support of this in the available literature, e.g., ***The Rich and the Rest of US***, by Tavis Smiley and Cornel West, Smiley Books [2012]. Both perspectives are the reasons that every country with the highest educational outcomes provides more supports for children and more programs to reduce poverty.

Much research has addressed the relationship between low education achievement and incarceration. There is also much research into the negative brain implications related to the stresses suffered by children living in poverty -- implications leading to behavioral, concentration and memory issues which impair one's ability to learn. It is, perhaps, easier to understand the dynamics of the 'cradle-to-prison' pipeline' originating in poverty.

The research draws a nexus between education and incarceration. Implied is the assumption low education achievement leads to a greater potential for incarceration. Implied is poor education is a cause of incarceration. The suggestion here is that inadequate educational outcomes are not a causation of incarceration but that the stresses of living in poverty and the neurological issues resulting from growing up in a non-nurturing environment are the causation of both the poor education outcomes for children living in poverty and the high rates of incarceration and recidivism as these children reach adulthood.

Although searched for, no research was uncovered implicating the brain development issues, particularly the executive function behavioral issues, and how these issues could lead to the criminal activity which, in turn, leads to incarceration. Were such research undertaken, it is believed that both the poor education outcomes and the criminal activity would have a nexus to stresses associated with growing up in a poverty environment and the subsequent brain damage.

As the Great Society programs of President Johnson proved, learning gaps can be reduced between lower and upper SES students. The Elementary and Secondary Education Act [1965], [R74] provided funds to support school programs for children in poverty. Head Start addressed learning gaps of children entering kindergarten. Other aspects of the Great Society addressed factors associated with poverty -- employment, housing, literacy and health care. Since the additional supports were removed, as America went through the 1980s and 1990s, the learning gaps have remained unchanged.

The revision of the Elementary and Secondary Education Act, in 1990, named No Child Left behind [NCLB], with its glowing rhetoric about bringing all children to the same learning achievement level by 2014, proved to be more of a detriment to the public education system than a source of support for children living in poverty. The basic premise behind NCLB is schools, alone, can overcome all of the negative impacts on a child's learning potential. One can cite current examples of states, that have been moving the 'target date' for implementation further out in years. In contrast to the 'glowing rhetoric' at the NCLB 'pep rallies', experience has clearly demonstrated that the NCLB advocates and promoters were seemingly unaware of the realities of education for children in poverty.

When subjected to federally supported standardized testing, low SES students consistently tested below higher SES students. As a result, under the NCLB school rating system, schools in high poverty neighborhoods were rated as 'failing'. No one, from the federal government down through the educational hierarchy, allowed for the connection between low student outcomes and high poverty. Although virtually all 'failing' schools were in high poverty areas, the schools were punished by threats of firing teachers and principals and closing the schools. Under its guidelines, the federal government insisted parents be told their child's school was 'failing' and be afforded the opportunity to attend 'alternate' schools -- the genesis of the charter school movement. That charter schools, although allowed many options not open to other public schools, have, on average, only achieved to the same levels as the schools they replaced is evidence that the underlying premise of NCLB that schools can overcome what poverty has created is a flawed premise. Diane Ravitch, United States Assistant secretary of Education and involved in the creation of NCLB, has become one of NCLB's harshest critics and a critic of the charter school movement.

Simply stated, the federal government set standards of achievement at a level appropriate for middle and upper class students. The federal government then required all students, regardless of the resources available to them, to achieve to those middle/upper class standards. Until recently, with the push for early childhood programs, the federal government has done virtually nothing to level the educational playing field for the children in poverty. The federal government failed to provide those resources already available to more affluent students at home -- resources that supplement and complement in-school learning and which account for significant numbers of points on standardized assessments. When, to no one's surprise, the children in poverty were unable to overcome their lack of resources -- schools, teachers and principals were blamed. This is how the federal government created 'failing' schools. When, in truth, the problem is a 'failing' federal government.

Hard to believe, with all the research indicating its potential, and the positive impact on America's fiscal well-being, addressing poverty in children has not only been ignored but derided. Even the current debate on minimum wages is telling. Increased minimum wages can have a profound impact on the well-being of a family with poorly educated parents unable to secure better paying jobs. Granted, increased minimum wages may mean that consumers will pay more for the fast food hamburger. However, wages that do not provide for basic needs force families to look for supplementary supports such as food programs, e.g., SNAP, food pantries, community food banks, free medical clinics or emergency rooms, and housing subsidies. All taxpayer subsidized supports. Either the consumer or the taxpayer is going to incur the cost. Which is the better choice? Increased wages are a positive incentive to be self-reliant. Government subsidies do exactly the opposite. Wages are a source of pride. Government hand-outs are a message that one is incapable of taking care of oneself or one's family and is an assault on personal pride.

That many of the poor do have pride and are embarrassed by hand-outs is evident in the school lunch program. The percentage of students receiving free/reduced price lunches is always lower at the high school level than in the younger grades - although records will show many of these high school students have siblings in lower grades who qualified for and are receiving the lunches. Older students would rather go hungry than be associated with the free lunch program.

In the discussion on a title for this book, the following title was suggested: *How to make Money from Poverty.* A country makes money from poverty by investing in its human capital, especially its children, to such an extent that poverty, with all its public costs and including the physical and mental costs to those who suffer poverty's impacts, is reduced to the lowest levels possible. America cannot afford to waste the potential of up to one quarter of its children by not addressing their needs. Bear in mind that these costs are increasing with time and are approaching the unsustainable level -- if not already there. The payback, however, via the early investment into children in poverty, is that addressing the needs in the short term reduces or even eliminates the needs in the long term.

Not addressing the needs generates costs -- costs for food and housing subsidies, medical care, and especially the huge incarceration outlays. Costs go on for infinity using current strategies. Investing, on the other hand, is a system of providing resources in the short term with the anticipation of returns on the investment in the long term. Unlike costs which, once spent, are gone forever, investments come back to the investor often returning more than the original investment -- even much more. Investing in our children creates more doctors, scientists, engineers, skilled technicians... and teachers. That is how one makes money from poverty or, more precisely, *from the elimination of poverty.*

LEARNING and TEACHING READINESS

In Section II, Introduction and Background, the dynamic relationship between 'learning' and 'teaching' and 'classroom management' requirements has been mentioned. Simply put, albeit that it may be a subtle point, is that 'learning readiness' and 'teaching readiness' must coincide for an efficient *and* meaningful educational process. Their coincidence in the classroom is a necessary and sufficient condition in order to minimize that time required for the 'classroom management' process. Of course, the more time devoted to classroom management translates directly to a comparable reduction in time available for the learning and teaching processes.

Ron Wolk [R25], former vice president of Brown University and a 2008 recipient of the Education Commission of the States' James Bryant Conant Award for his outstanding contribution to American Education has provided a much-needed perspective on the impact of the 'readiness' spectrum upon the flawed belief that, education wise, "one size fits all"! Another credible message is provided by Marian Wright Edelman's Child Watch Column -- especially, in the June 2015 article entitled *'Growing Seeds for a Multicultural, Multiracial Teaching Force for Our Rainbow Children'.* This particular publication sheds light upon some of poverty's dimensions: emotional poverty, a poverty of love, mental poverty and social poverty. Another way of expressing their thoughts is that the total educational arena -- not just the classical and conventional school arenas -- is in critical need for educational programs, protocols and curricula that are shaped to the needs of the specific student population. As the ethnic diversity and impacts of poverty vary, then the statement "one size doesn't fit all" seems to make a lot of common sense. Also, the practice of "one size does fit all" pursued by educational administrators and educational 'engineers' may just be a contributing factor -- even a significant factor -- for having left behind countless children and their opportunity to move forward.

It is widely recognized and acknowledged that America's traditional and historical educational process from pre-K, primary grades, middle school, high school, college academics and acceptable alternative training programs has been uniquely successful for those students who have the experience and benefits of 'preparation', i.e. for those families, teachers and children removed from the impact of a sustained poverty. An integral part of this traditional and historical 'success story' is that this particular successful educational process is best characterized by a sequential preparatory, i.e., aka 'readiness', *process* that enables a relatively smooth transition through the overall educational process. A process that has long enjoyed a comparable high level of teaching readiness! But what of those families and children who are born into a poverty stricken environment -- and those teachers who simply are not prepared for being successful teachers in those schools reflecting the inequalities of a sustained poverty -- where 'readiness' is not a priority and not always a reality...an environment that is a virtual prison with life sentences... what happens to them? It is acknowledged that the former educational arena will continue on its constantly evolving path of success; however, the latter educational arena poses significant challenges for both teachers, students and their families! Is it possible that these two educational arenas have very different 'teaching and learning readiness requirements'... and, perhaps, very different budget/funding requirements? An interesting question!

The relevance of 'preparation' is universally recognized as an entity necessary for 'success' in any endeavor but, at this point' we are looking at the role of 'preparation' [aka 'readiness'] for its role *throughout one's educational journey...and beyond!* There is an abundance of literature addressing 'readiness' especially in early childhood policy and practice, e.g. [R59], [R60], [R79a]. There are also efforts addressing primary school readiness, e.g., [R80], which points out that the 'focus of Primary School preparation' is not so much academic but rather, more importantly, that the student can communicate, move and socialize. Readiness for Middle School is also addressed, e.g., [R81], [R82]; the former touched upon the linkage between high school performance and earlier grades, especially middle school grades. The latter addresses the linkage between the lack of middle school readiness/preparation and 'the high rates of high school dropouts and low rates of college readiness'. The point is also made that the transition from middle school to high school depends on the cognitive and behavioral skills developed earlier. High school readiness also draws a lot of attention, e.g. [R83]; specifically, this Applied Survey Research report [2007] identifies the importance and relevance of 'metrics' in its High School Outcomes Project entitled "*How well did we prepare our students for "life after high school?"* This educational 'journey' includes 'college readiness', e.g., [R84], [R85], and, then, employment readiness, e.g., [R86]. The theme of this latter reference reminds the readers of an important responsibility, i.e., 'College Readiness and Life Skills: Moving Beyond Academics.'

Let's look at Figure 6, Readiness Dynamics for the 'Prepared ' and 'Unprepared'. This dichotomization certainly maintains the continuing success for those who are 'prepared' for the sequential educational process.

The outcome for these students is the time-proven transition to employment, upward mobility, income stability, family stability, becoming societal contributors, etc. Like all processes and experiences, education has two possible outcomes, *i.e., the well recognized 'successful' one and then the not so well recognized 'unsuccessful' one!* The latter group of students from the various strata of poverty -- for a variety of rationales and reasons -- are basically 'unprepared' for a minimally, even reasonably, successful journey through their educational process. Again, the question must be asked, "What happens to them?" A small percentage of these students are able to 'reenter' the traditional and very successful educational process. Most, though, enter a lifetime of residence within unemployment, low wages, poverty and all its derivatives, i.e., the spectrum of inequities, lack of resources, instabilities, etc.

Having provided some thoughts on 'readiness' citing some representative references from the reservoir of educational references, it may be appropriate to refer to Appendix A, 'Systems Prologue', i.e., the view of a situation via a systems [wide angle] lens rather than focusing on a 'piece' of the situation provides an invaluable perspective and enables an analytical leveraging process.

Figures 7 and 8 provide a very representative list of *readiness factors* and a composite *readiness model and its linkages* and *dynamics*. Figure 9 provides the spectrum of inequalities likely experienced by those prime candidates, i.e., the *unprepared* identified in Figure 6. However, Figure 10 provides some interesting insight into the unique linkage between the chain of critical educational readiness factors and the spectrum of outcomes, i.e., the inequalities. Although the weights for each element have time-based and location-based variations, they clearly convey a strong inference [1] that each inequality factor is not a one-to-one function with any particular single readiness factor but rather impacts a composite function of a set of readiness factors and [2] that, conversely, each readiness factor can impact most inequality factors to some degree. The weight of each element could be a value, a single or multivariable function or a statistical distribution, e.g., Gaussian. The purpose of Figure 10 is to enhance the awareness that we are dealing with a complex and convoluted situation [primarily due to the multitude of linkages which may be linear or nonlinear] or as Peter Edelman offers in *So Rich, So Poor* [R21]: "Everything is connected to everything!"

The spreadsheet/matrix of Figure 10 clearly demonstrates and emphasizes that *'indeed, everything is connected to everything'*! It is important to note **that these linkages between educational readiness factors [Figures 7 and 8]** and **inequalities** [Figure 9] *can* yield/enable both '+' as well as '-' outcomes.

The numbers in each of the cells of this spreadsheet represent the 'intensity' of the impact of a specific inequality upon a specific educational readiness factor. Specifically, the site-specific numbers shown reflect current conditions and their detrimental impacts upon those educational readiness factors of Figures 7 and 8 for those living with these poverty-driven inequalities. **It is critically important to always remember that education is the unique key to transition**

Colella & Crowley

from the despair of poverty to opportunity and an enhanced quality of life.

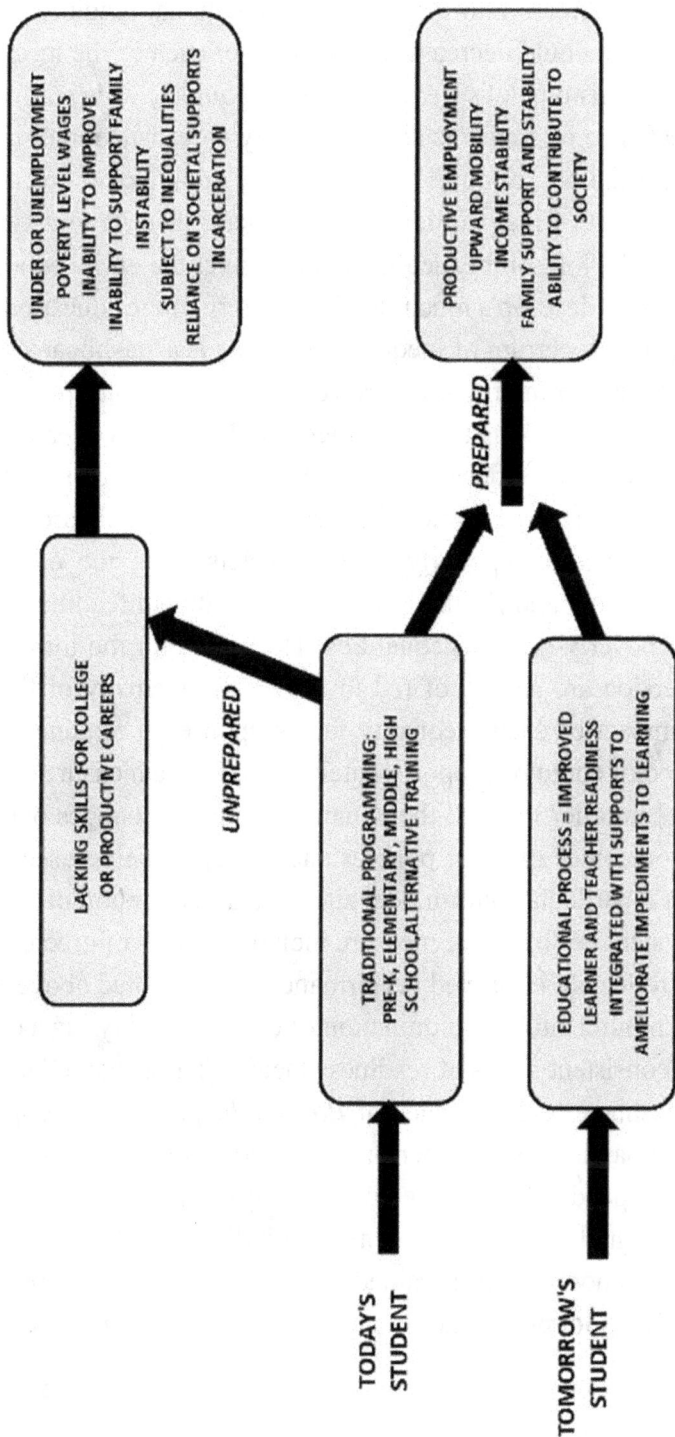

FIGURE 6 - READINESS DYNAMICS FOR THE 'PREPARED' AND THE 'UNPREPARED.'

It is interesting to note that the educational readiness factors, when realized, could decrease the intensity of each of the inequalities of Figure 9; this type of spreadsheet [or its equivalent] is really a two-way street. The inference is that a corollary spreadsheet/matrix could also reflect the education-driven reduction, minimization or, ideally, the elimination of inequalities. The argument, then, is to reverse the mastery of the long-imbedded inequalities over the entire educational process and to develop a much-needed mastery of the educational process over this spectrum of inequalities. There is a 'dashboard' version of the spreadsheet/matrix of Figure 10 at *Poverty-Inequalities.com*. Either version is a tracking tool for either '+' or '-' <u>*changes*</u> over a timeline of years and, perhaps, decades in direct response to program initiatives and their outcomes over time. The website-based 'dashboard' versions reflect [1] historical poverty-driven impacts upon the educational readiness factors and [2] the impacts of educational readiness factors upon the poverty-driven inequalities. The colors for the former dashboard version are shades of red to reflect the intensity of the detrimental impact of each inequality factor upon each readiness factor. The red color could be proportionately shaded [as a measure of impact intensity] in order to track the dynamics, i.e., the changes over time, that are outcomes of those policies and strategies being used and assessed at a particular pilot-model site. The latter version of this composite system performance measure includes shades of green as a 2nd color to reflect an improved performance, i.e., as noted above, the reduction, minimization or elimination of each inequality via a continuous and consistent series of readiness factors. These exemplary color-coded 'dashboards' are located at *Poverty-Inequalities.com* and provides a dynamic 'systems' performance indicator comparable to that cited in Appendix B. By inference, this **system metric**, by virtue of tracking '+' and '-' outcomes, is also an indicator of 'what's working' and 'what is not' -- each a valued input to program planning, e.g., a site-specific pilot project, and an efficient budgeting process.

READINESS MODEL COMPONENTS/HIERARCHY

RF-1: PRE-NATAL READINESS [MOTHER, CHILD]

RF-2: HEALTH CARE READINESS [MOTHER, CHILD]

RF-3: CONSISTENT FAMILY ADVOCACY AND SUPPORT READINESS [PUBLIC & PRIVATE SECTORS

RF-4: PRE-K LEARNING & READINESS

RE-5: GRADES K-3 LEARNING & READINESS

RF-6: GRADES 4-8 LEARNING & READINESS

RF-7: GRADES 9-12 LEARNING & READINESS

RF-8: ALTERNATIVE EDUCATION LEARNING & READINESS

RF-9: COLLEGE TEACHING & LEARNING READINESS

RF-10: LIFE SKILLS READINESS

RF-11: TECHNOLOGY & LITERACY READINESS

RF-12: EMPLOYMENT READINESS

RF-13: CAREER/UPWARD MOBILITY READINESS

RF-14: SOCIETAL PARTICIPATION/ACCEPTANCE READINESS

RF-15: TEACHING READINESS [throughout EDUCATIONAL PROCESS]

RF-16: ADVOCACY & SUPPORT [throughout RF-1. RF-2,... RF-15]

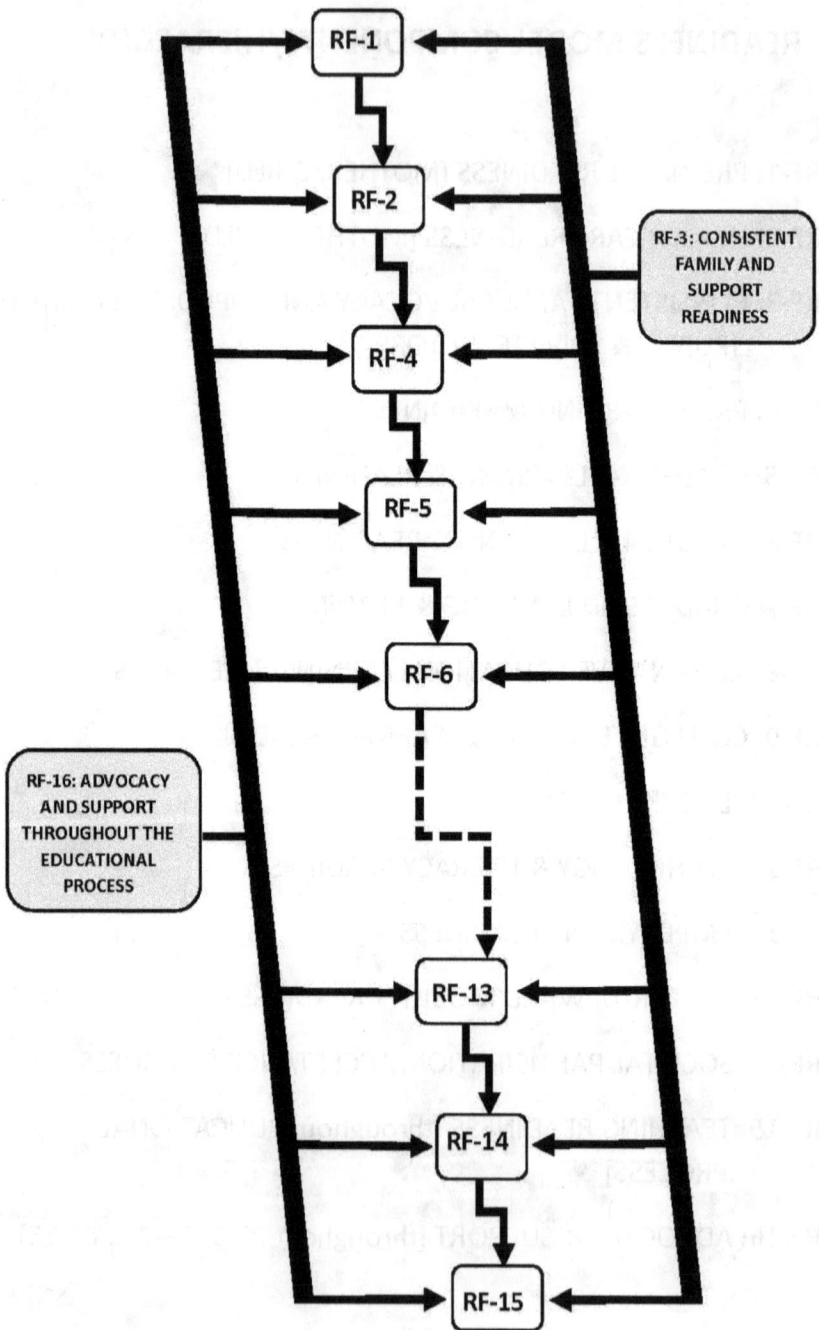

FIGURE 8 - READINESS MODEL LINKAGE/DYNAMICS

DEFINITIONS FOR INEQUALITIES: INEQ-1 - INEQ-20

INEQ-1: EDUCATION

INEQ-2: INSUFFICIENT READINESS

INEQ-3: FAMILY, COMMUNITY & ORGANIZATIONAL ADVOCACY & SUPPORT

INEQ-4: BEYOND ACADEMICS [ART, MUSIC, THEATER, ETC.]

INEQ-5: HOUSING

INEQ-6: ACCESS TO MEDICAL CARE

INEQ-7: HEALTH

INEQ-8: LIFE SKILLS

INEQ-9: EMPLOYMENT

INEQ-10: KNOWLEDGE OF AND ACCESS TO SOCIAL SERVICES

INEQ-11: TRANSPORTATION

INEQ-12: UPWARD MOBILITY

INEQ-13: JUSTICE SYSTEM/ACCESS TO LEGAL COUNSEL

INEQ-14: INCOME

INEQ-15: 'VOICE'

INEQ-16: COMPASSION/HUMANITARIAN PERSPECTIVE

INEQ-17: DOMESTIC/STREET VIOLENCE

INEQ-18: ADAPTIVE STRATEGIES FOR THOSE WHO FALL 'THROUGH THE CRACK IN FLOORS' OF THE OVERALL EDUCATIONAL READINESS FACTORS

INEQ-19: CONSISTENT AND CONTINUING ACCOUNTABILITY FOR THE ADAPTIVE STRATEGIES OF **INEQ-18**

INEQ-20: OVERALL 'QUALITY OF LIFE'

EDUCATIONAL READINESS FACTORS
AND THEIR LINKAGES TO EACH INEQUALITY

	RF-1	RF-2	RF-3	RF-4	RF-5	RF-6	RF-7	RF-8	RF-9	RF-10	RF-11	RF-12	RF-13	RF-14	RF-15	RF-16
INEQ-1	4	4	4	8	8	8	10	9	10	10	8	9	9	10	8	10
INEQ-2	7	7	5	9	10	10	10	8	10	8	8	9	9	9	9	8
INEQ-3	7	7	7	7	7	7	7	7	7	7	7	7	7	7	7	7
INEQ-4	3	3	3	3	3	5	5	6	7	7	7	6	6	6	8	8
INEQ-5	5	5	5	6	6	7	7	7	8	8	8	8	9	9	10	10
INEQ-6	10	10	10	10	10	10	10	10	10	10	10	10	10	10	10	10
INEQ-7	10	10	8	5	5	5	5	5	5	7	7	8	8	8	10	9
INEQ-8	7	7	7	7	7	8	8	8	9	10	8	9	9	9	9	9
INEQ-9	4	4	4	4	4	4	6	6	6	8	8	9	9	9	9	9
INEQ-10	9	9	10	7	7	7	7	9	9	10	9	9	9	9	10	10
INEQ-11	2	2	2	5	5	5	5	8	9	9	9	9	10	8	10	10
INEQ-12	5	5	5	8	8	8	8	9	9	9	9	9	10	8	10	10
INEQ-13	2	2	6	3	4	5	6	9	7	10	8	8	8	9	9	10
INEQ-14	3	3	4	5	5	5	5	9	9	10	9	9	9	9	9	9
INEQ-15	8	8	8	8	8	8	8	8	8	9	9	9	9	9	9	9
INEQ-16	8	8	8	8	8	8	8	8	8	10	9	9	10	10	10	10
INEQ-17	3	3	8	4	4	4	8	9	9	10	8	9	9	9	9	10
INEQ-18	9	9	9	9	9	9	9	9	9	9	9	9	9	9	9	9
INEQ-19	9	9	9	9	9	9	9	9	9	9	9	9	9	9	9	9
INEQ-20	10	10	10	10	10	10	10	10	10	10	10	10	10	10	10	10

FIGURE 10 - RELATIVE IMPACTS* OF READINESS FACTORS
AND INEQUALITIES UPON EACH OTHER

* These weights are representative; actual weights will be poverty-site specific within any pilot project and its assessment.

Let us give some thought to the following:

[1] The costs associated with the education of the 'prepared' students of Figure 6 are significant, necessary and increasing with the passage of time.

[2] The educators of the 'prepared' students are providing a quite remarkable 'teaching' performance despite those challenges mandated by the educational administrators and 'engineers.'

[3] The costs associated with the education of the 'unprepared' and those outcomes that result directly from their 'unpreparedness' is increasing [perhaps, exponentially] with the passage of time.

These particular costs do have a marginal positive impact but, for for the most part, are really *'maintenance costs'* for the status quo.

Specifically, the return on these costs [ROI] associated with [3] are minimal [compared to the ROI/investment costs associated with [1]. The costs of [3] are viewed by many as necessary "maintenance' costs, although ineffective with regard to social progress with little, if any, regard for their associated [ROI].

[4] Putting it another way, there is progress with [1] and [2] but really minimal progress with [3].

[5] Whereas the costs of [1] are measured in budget $$$; however, the costs of [3] are also measured in budget $$$ costs with little, if any regard for the humanitarian, opportunity and quality of life costs [each priceless]. The *'real costs of poverty are addressed in Appendix C as well as at Poverty-Inequalities.com.*

[6] Some insight into applying Life Cycle Cost [LCC], [RC-5], analysis to [3] [rather than current conventional annual budgeting procedures] *and* prioritizing

progress [as measured by a continuing reduction... minimization... elimination of 'inequalities] yields not only a dramatic decrease in LCC but also an equally dramatic increase in the return on the investment of LCC 'up-front budgeting'. LCC are addressed in greater detail in Appendix C.

[7] Those individuals, agencies, organizations et al that -- quietly and effectively -- provide support, advocacy, 'voice', services, compassion et al are doing more than a remarkable job with minimal and decreasing budgets in the face of constantly increasing client bases and their spectrum of needs.

[8] This section is entitled ***Learning and Teaching Readiness***. The former, 'learning readiness' has been addressed whereas the latter, 'teaching readiness', was briefly mentioned in Section I and characterized as a necessary companion to learning residence. Each are necessary for an effective educational process to exist; alone neither are sufficient but, together, their synergism provides sufficiency. Let's look at Figure 6 again; the dichotomization of 'students' into those who are 'prepared' and those who are 'unprepared' highlights that, for the most part, learning and teaching readiness enjoy classroom residence, for the 'prepared' students. However, this co-existence of learning and teaching readiness, for the most part, is more difficult -- sometimes, extremely difficult for 'unprepared students' in any one of a variety of disabling and challenging educational environments, e.g., that growing student population in which 'one size doesn't fit all' applies, out-of-school students, lack of real-world skills, unemployment, on-the-street, dysfunctional associations, criminal activities, incarceration, mental disabilities et al. As mentioned earlier in the beginning text of this Section,

Learning and Teaching Readiness, it is important to note that the educational needs for this latter group are significantly different for those students who are 'prepared'! A major component of their educational needs that cries for attention lies in the acquisition of life skills; again, it is important to note the 'one size doesn't fit all' - a paradigm that is applicable to all educational processes.

Chapter VI
Poverty Model

C oncerned individuals, over the last six or seven decades, have long cried out that "Something must be done!" with follow-on echoes of *"What can be be done?"* and *"What should be done?"* A prerequisite for answering these questions is to have an understanding and acknowledgement of the realities of poverty and its inequalities. The same is true for the world of education. Currently the linkage between poverty and education is the impact of poverty-driven inequalities upon the spectrum of of educational arenas.

In order to achieve a meaningful level of understanding, there is the requirement to have a meaningful representation of poverty, education and its network of linkages as a starting point!

The beginnings of a representation [aka 'model'] of the world of poverty is initially addressed in Section V. Specifically, Figure 2 shows the basic elements of the 'system of poverty' in canonical form, i.e., a system that is innately dynamic with the passage of time. Figure 4 shows the 'clusters' of linkages that provide a more comprehensive view of the network of the world of poverty. Both figures also delineate the spectrum of poverty-driven inequalities.

Although Figures 2 and 4 infer an expanding representation, the authors have developed a significantly more expansive model of poverty. This expansion [and a similar one for education] requires a website complement to the book text to meet the requirements for an understanding of poverty [and education] and their linkages that give rise to a convoluted and complex network]. This website, ***Poverty-Inequalities.com,*** provides the users the navigational capability that is necessary to follow the development of the more comprehensive models for poverty and education ***and*** their dynamic relationship. Each of these models, then, serve as **inputs to a cost model** that yields the total and true costs of poverty -- costs that are becoming **unsustainable**.

Poverty-Inequalities.com provides, for the readers and website users, a compendium of the website features and an informative introduction to the use of the website.

The website features and goals follow:

- Enable awareness and acknowledgement of poverty that is unfair, undeserved, unnecessary and unacceptable.
- The still continuing growth of poverty inflicts an unsustainable cost in dollars, opportunity and the quality of life as well as the intangible costs beyond dollars.
- This growing -- and unsustainable aggregation of costs is seriously amplified by poverty-driven inequalities.
- Why does poverty still exist and continue to grow?
- Poverty has a catastrophic effect upon the educational arena.
- Yet relief of poverty lies in the educational arena.
- What can be done? What should be done?
- Provides some 'food for thought' for a foundational, systemic methodology so necessary for the development of candidate solutions.
- Consider this user-friendly navigational capability for an ***experiential journey through the valley of poverty*** and its companion, the educational arena, and its immeasurable costs to all Americans.

Chapter VII
Education Model

As noted in Section VI, there is a similarity between the requirements for the poverty representation and that of the education representation. However, it is the education model that also captures the critical linkage between poverty and education... and the impacts of one upon the other.

The education model, as has been done for the poverty model, has its genesis with its canonical structure of Figure 3; it is also a dynamic model that varies with the passage of time. Figure 5, with its many 'clusters', shows an expanded view of the education model.

But first, some perspective: let's imagine that poverty in America simply did not exist. It follows that the spectrum of poverty-driven inequalities would also be non-existent. It then follows that the catastrophic impact of these inequalities upon the growing spectrum of educational arenas would not exist either. Again, it follows that the entire spectrum of student populations would be the beneficiaries of a sound, meaningful and relevant education that, as history has demonstrated, would really 'level the playing field' for all, not just some!

However, Figure 6 reflects the realities of life; specifically, that, for the most part, those who are 'prepared' within the traditional or conventional educational hierarchies are thus well equipped for employment, upward mobility and a very acceptable quality of life. They, the 'prepared', essentially, have an immunity to poverty-driven inequalities. Conversely, those who are 'unprepared,' e.g., those living in poverty, don't have this immunity but rather inherit unemployment, low wages, poverty, instability, incarceration and an unacceptable quality of life.

'Prepared' or 'unprepared' is a direct derivative of one's 'readiness' for education throughout the spectrum of educational processes, i.e., those within the conventional and those outside of the conventional educational arenas. As we all recognize that "Ready or not, here comes life!" Figure 7 provides a likely list of readiness factors; the readiness dynamics of Figure 8 demonstrate the necessity of the continuity of advocacy and support and the consistency of family and support throughout the chain of educational processes. Figure 9, provides a list of the poverty-driven [major] inequalities. Figure 10 provides the two way cause-and-effect relationship between inequalities and readiness factors. This particular relationship is brought to life on the website via some revealing graphics. Additionally, this format leads to a much needed and effective site-specific metric for progress and the lack of progress, within both the poverty and educational arenas.

Poverty-Inequalities.com provides, like the poverty model of Section VI, an expanded, more comprehensive educational model has been developed, and, like the expanded poverty model of Section VI, requires this website complement. The website's navigational capability enables the users to follow the development of the more comprehensive models for both poverty and education and, most importantly, their unique and dynamic relationship. The authors respectfully recommend that the website users experience their website 'journeys, through both the poverty and educational models. Both models, then, merge within a cost model that yields the total and true costs of poverty -- both the dollar costs and the aggregate of intangible costs for which we all pay. The website also offers the opportunity to directly interact with the authors!

Chapter VIII
A Pilot Model: The Next 'First Step'

There is no shortage of 'models' that, collectively, provide a wide spectrum of interests, concerns, perspectives and levels of experience and expertise. Some representative and relevant models have already been mentioned here, e.g., [R26], [R27], [R51], [R52], [R87], [R88] and especially [R89] which certainly exemplifies the 'flavor' of that necessary direction that needs to be taken in order to enable a meaningful and sustainable solution. Specifically, Ambrose [R89] comments about a 'new idea' to address persistent and heart rending social issues effectively and with cost-efficiency; he also reminds us of the Congress's track record of developing and maintaining a 'system that has provided too little for far too much.' Additionally, Ambrose reminds his readers that 'the Congress [historically] figures it has the final answer to something it clearly knows little about, it then combines political conniving with good intentions and it delivers maybe just a portion of the intended consequences along with some harmful unintended ones'. One might even sense the relevance between Ambrose's observations and the overall message of this document!

This 'new idea', entitled Pay for Success [aka 'social income bonds'], has its genesis in the United Kingdom [UK] and has been applied both in Australia and America, e.g., reaching out to the private sector to manage social services and/or educational programs. Funding will be obtained from investors; returns on this investment will not be forthcoming from the government until an independent accountability process has been completed and verified. *Interestingly enough, the claim is that this methodology <u>could</u> be used at the federal, state and local levels using 'scalability'* [Appendix B] to address a wide spectrum of social issues, e.g., homelessness, school dropouts, recidivism, etc. Some current efforts to privatize educational and social services in America may be identified as similar efforts; however, the current function of accountability, i.e., an independent verification of the service providers' performance *prior to* payment for those services need some serious improvements and, then, continuous updating.

However, the verification process [as a pre-requisite for payment] could be time-consuming and the performance and cost effectiveness during that duration of time for verification would really represent an unnecessary risk to both the effort but, more importantly, to the recipients of those educational and social services; however, the risk of not including accountability [as is the current practice] as an integral part of the solution presents a far greater and continuing risk.

Ambrose's closing statements are both noteworthy and impressive, i.e., that there exists the possibility that could lead to less societal disadvantages, less crime, less unemployment and more. However, the realization of this attractive possibility *'will obviously require more than Pay for Success'!*

Lee H. Hamilton, Director of the Center for Congress at Indiana University and also a former member of the United States House of Representatives for 34 years offers a poignant perspective in *Why government fails and what we must do about it* [R90]. His perspective may initially be 'heard' as a criticism but further thought would reveal that it is a very constructive and forward-looking one. Simply put, his comments are really a reflection of the necessity for true critical analysis in any arena. A critical analysis process is necessary for progress, performance effectiveness and cost-efficiency; this process [to paraphrase an earlier statement]: "What's working?" and "What's not working?" are pre-requisites for moving forward.

Hamilton puts forth six candidate 'fixes' for 'politicians to consider to improve government management and policy implementation:

- Ensure that federal agencies use *pilot and trial programs* much more frequently than they do now.
- Mandate more rigorous evaluation procedures [remember accountability!] **and the use of metrics.**
- Avoid the rush to announce programs, 'get it right rather than get it quickly... think about *long-term, not the next election,* and make sure the **mission goal is clearly defined.**
- Reduce the number of [most] political appointees in favor of individuals with relevant experience and a demonstrated expertise.
- Reduce the bureaucratic hierarchies so that the 'view from the top' is realistic and not bureaucracy filtered.
- Hamilton, very directly, states, "In the case of Congress, it needs to ensure that *vigorous oversight* of programs becomes a habit, not the rarity it is now." [Although Congress often practices its oversight function in a matter-after-the-fact style, a common scenario is a congressional hearing involving enthusiastic questioning of those individuals responsible for a particular issue, program or problem often followed by the resignation of those same individuals]. This latent oversight, however, often sheds light upon a political appointee who has a flawed sense and grasp of responsibility and accountability. However, *vigorous oversight* must be an integral part of the planning, designing, development, operation, maintenance and budgeting processes rather than a matter-after-the-fact!

Pilot models are both necessary and useful in order to establish
[1] a further shaping [aka 'fine-tuning'] of a specific program and, most importantly,

[2] the increased measure of program feasibility prior to the budgeting and expenditure of funds for a program of greater scope. Simply put, a pilot model addresses the **'proof of concept'** requirement. Additionally, the pilot model offers the opportunity to determine the validity of specific processes within the solution concept, e.g., the applicability of life cycle cost [LCC] to a societal issue.

The literature is rich in the advantages and risks of related efforts, e.g., [R25], [R52], [R53], [R59], [R87], [R88], and [R89]. There are however, two references, when taken together, provide an attractive view of the future. First, [RB-3] is an effort from the United Kingdom of a pilot model in place to assist in the development of government plans and policies to address the needs of needy and disadvantaged [for whatever reason] populations. It is important to note that the rationale for this 'prototype/pilot' model is to obtain **real-world credibility and reliable guidance and direction for the expenditure of resources, i.e., government funds, time, experience and expertise, etc.** Hopefully, this rationale strikes a resonance with the readers of this document. Reference has been previously made to [RB-3] as a methodology that certainly provides the 'flavor' of a solution. Secondly, [R52] refers to the need for an arena to plan, implement and evaluate strategies to address poverty. In fact, anti-poverty activist Sister Simone [R58], at the 2014 Rhode Island Interfaith Coalition to Reduce Poverty at its 6th annual conference on poverty, emphatically stated "In Rhode Island **you have an amazing opportunity. You are small enough** and could be the petri dish for our nation to show a positive way forward." The planning, design, development, implementation and continuing assessment of a pilot model is not a simple task; however, the pilot model process must respond to a set of validated requirements. Hamilton [R90] has already provided guidance in that area: the pilot model must include metrics and an accountability function, long-term thinking and, yes, vigorous [continuing] oversight as pre-requisites for credible, extrapolated real-world outcomes. Again, the pilot model is a 'proof of concept' process. It is a process through which the questions: 'What's working?' and 'What's not working? or, more specifically, 'What will probably work?' and 'What will probably not work?' are answered with varying degrees of uncertainty [aka 'risk'].

The duration of time [and the associated resources] to use the pilot model strategy/methodology varies with the dynamics ['changes with time'] of the pilot model behavior. Let us remember that the social and political inertia of poverty et al populations are almost immeasurable and the identification and behavior of their respective [s-l-o-w moving] dynamics will take time. These dynamics must be identified via the tracking of **appropriate and credible metrics**. One of the challenging, but absolutely necessary, requirements for the pilot model is its resonance to the poverty and education models of Section VI and VII. The selection of a site for a pilot model must also have a demonstrated resonance with these poverty and education models.

A necessary corollary to a decision to initiate the pilot model is its program planning process. A detailed program plan starting with pilot model requirements through its 'outcomes' [revisit Figure 1] includes implementation strategies, decision-making, i.e., the triad of responsibility, authority and accountability, resources, detailed plan for the testing hierarchy, data acquisition for on-going measurement & assessment to enable the success and relevance of the pilot model process.

Together, both the pilot model and the program plan would be necessary guidance for pilot models at other sites. As in the educational arena, the flawed proposition that 'one size fits all' also applies to site-specific pilot models and program planning and implementation. However, as in education, there will be a factor of commonality amongst the site-specific pilot models and their program planning and implementation. The sequence of multiple pilot models is a prelude to a national program commitment to ending poverty.

Chapter IX
The Choices Ahead

Preamble to Choices

The initial thoughts of the authors of this section were to provide a clear concise comprehensive summary of those items in the Executive Summary, perhaps, a paragraph or so on each item. However, this is a *fait accompli* as these items and this book, per se, are really a mutually supportive duality.

Historically, the foundation of sound, relevant and meaningful decisions are based on recognized and accepted principles, using information [as opposed to 'noise', e.g., news and social media chatter], and, most importantly, the awareness of the requirement to innately embrace a compassionate and humanitarian perspective. These type of decisions , inevitably, yield positive outcomes for all those involved, i.e., the decision-makers, the administration hierarchy *and* especially all those impacted by the decision: those in need and aka 'clients'. One does not have to search too far to discover a historical and current litany of decisions that have lacked a compassionate and humanitarian perspective. The driving force behind these types of decisions are usually [1] a thirst for power [personal, financial, military et al], [2] fear and/or a lack of information and foresight and, simply put , a blatant regard for those impacted by a decision.

Both the former and the latter decision-making processes yield very contrasting *consequences* and, very much like all decision processes, the decision-makers bear the responsibility for those decisions made. Is this not what we teach our children, i.e., that every decision made has a consequence for which they are responsible. *The most meaningful measure of any decision is the outcome[s] of that decision with the passage of time.* 'Good' decisions, inevitably, enable positive and lasting outcomes. 'Poor' decisions? Well, the alternative outcome is the inevitable and lasting damage inflicted upon humanity via irresponsibility, e.g., a lack of foresight,-intended or not!

A guiding light in any decision process is 'what is the right thing to do?' The answer to this question does always come easily and readily to some but not all. The 'right thing to do' is an integral part of any decision-making process at all levels of activity: personal, family, community, school, administration, the political arena, the military arena, government, health et al. A local school example: a school superintendent [R91] made the decision to place all of the elementary-age children from a recently opened shelter for homeless families into district schools. The fearful and negative reaction from the parents of children in those schools protested via a somewhat uninformed and compassionless perspective. This reaction brings back memories of the resistance of the 1960s to school integration... and we all know the inevitable outcome to a policy that was blatantly *unfair, undeserved, unnecessary and unacceptable.* In that experience, the closing statement [by the school superintendent] of the cited reference [R91] is noteworthy: " ...and I will do what I believe is the right thing to do." Let's also remember Andrew Goodman, James Earl Chaney and Michael Schwerner [R92]. They were the three civil rights activists who were murdered by members of the Ku Klux Klan on June 21, 1964. The civil rights efforts during that time were challenging, chaotic and very dangerous! These three gentlemen -- recipients of the Presidential Medal of Freedom in November 2014 -- epitomized the willingness of countless others from all walks of American life to "do the right thing." They made their decision to travel from New York to Mississippi to facilitate voter registration for African-Americans and to advocate for their constitutional rights. However, they paid with their lives which were certainly not in vain but rather made a huge difference in the lives of so many-then, now and in the future. Each of these -- of a myriad -- examples underscore the relevance of compassion and humanitarianism as a necessary component of the decision process.

An important part of the continuing and proud legacy of America is that cadre of individuals who willingly made the decision to "do the right thing" throughout our American history. Within the civil rights arena, [R93] recalls the lives of Dr. Vincent Harding, Dr. Martin Luther King, Jr., John Siegenthaler and John Doar who passed away in 2014 but 'left us a much better people and nation'. As did Andrew Goodman, James Earl Chaney and Michael Schwerner did fifty years earlier!

The message for humanitarianism and compassion for all continues to surface, e.g., Dr. Martin Luther King, Jr. [R4], James Patterson [R15], Daniel Patrick Moynihan [R16], Mario Matthew Cuomo [R94], If not "US," then "Who?" If not "Now," then "When?"

Out of clutter, find simplicity. From discord, find harmony.
In the middle of difficulty, lies opportunity.
~Albert Einstein

Choices...

Perhaps, the first choice to be made by the readers is to reflect [or not] upon the message and theme of this book and the website and, if so, ask the following questions:

- "Is this message relevant?"
- "Does it embrace the principles of common sense?"
- "Does it embrace the principle of humanitarianism? ...of compassion?"
- "Does it make a reasonable argument for long-term financial planning, integrity and accountability?"

- "Is it feasible/reasonable to provide a meaningful response to the spectrum of continuing and growing spectrum of poverty-driven inequalities?"
- "Do these inequalities call for action, a national mandate?" ...a financial mandate? ...a moral mandate?

Another choice would be to visit the referenced website [of Sections VI and VII] to reflect upon the possibilities of 'doing the right thing, the responsible thing' and to further understand the reason and rationale for a systemic approach.

Still another choice -- for some -- would be to do nothing differently which only serves to perpetuate the **unfair, undeserved, unnecessary, unacceptable** current world of poverty and its inequalities. **Unsustainable costs** in a growing debt [waiting to come due sooner or later] in terms of budget and the quality of life is also a collateral reality of this choice.

Of course, there also exists the choice to be a naysayer. a charter member of the status quo club or even to remain in denial based on fear, innate reluctance, a blindness to humanity [R2] or a lack of political courage [aka timidity]. That is a choice that will be made by some but not all. Within that context, history has demonstrated, abundantly, that the greatness of America has **always** been achieved despite the naysayers et al who really made America's road longer and more arduous and so much more costly both in dollars , lost opportunities and the priceless intangibles of life. The greatness of America achieved in the past 238 years did not depend upon the actions of the naysayers et al but the true believers and practitioners of that founding document called the Constitution which, not incidentally, embraced all Americans not just some! In similar fashion the future inevitable greatness of America will also fall upon the shoulders of the latter group. Thank God!

The quality of **'greatness exists at all levels of the American landscape"** but it is quite ironic -- but still great and inspirational -- that those without reasonable position, authority, budget and influence continue daily in the trenches of society to 'make a difference in the lives of others' and each and all are to be acknowledged and commended for all that they do: usually under difficult and often, unnecessary circumstances. Conversely, the initial quality of American greatness was uniquely provided by our founding fathers who did overcome their differences by understanding that theirs was a ***national responsibility***. Over the recent years and political administrations, the Congressional leadership has eroded into an arena of political posturing, ideological [and often irrelevant and useless] bickering, alliances with political action groups, 'insider' activities, vested and special interests, personal political and financial gain, etc. This erosion has steadily migrated to Congressional 'gridlock' [R95] while their responsibilities are sidestepped.

This 'gridlock' has been abundantly fueled by those politicians who apparently have put their biases, self-interests and party ideologies above and beyond their American responsibilities.

This critique clearly is not applicable to all members of the Congress and State legislatures so there may still be hope for greatness. In the past, we have rallied with cries of "Remember the Alamo." "Remember the Maine." "Remember Pearl Harbor." and, more recently "Remember 9/11," perhaps, "Remember the Constitution" and "Remember the people, all the people" could be added to this list of remembrances.

Having said that which has been said for more than a few pages, i.e., there is a critical and important choice to be made between the 'status quo' and, perhaps, doing something. "Something must be done!" is the rallying cry of the 20th century; again, reference is made to [R4], [R15], [R16], [R94] and more. These same cries for equality for all and not just some are still heard in the 21st century! This book and its companion website offers, minimally, some 'food for thought and reflection' and, perhaps, just perhaps, future action in its recommendation for a pilot program. The planning process for a pilot program that is very likely feasible and with very promising outcomes and, therefore, is certainly well worth the effort to ascertain the feasibility of doing something that is absolutely necessary at a reasonable cost.

In section VIII, *A Pilot Model: The Next 'First' Step*, the relevance and rationale for a pilot model was provided. The development of this pilot model, then, is the next step; this will entail the following:

[1] Subject the pilot model process to a critical review process; this process includes questions [and answers] about the model development, structure and dynamics as well as the utility and meaningfulness of model outcomes.

[2] Access to this critical review will be provided to all interested parties via a user friendly interactive website currently being developed by the Innovative and Design Laboratory at the School of Engineering and Design at Johnson & Wales University.

[3] Based on the results of [1] and [2], finalize the validated requirements for the pilot model.

[4] Develop a selection criteria for the site[s] of the pilot model.

[5] Determine the pilot model 'team' which includes committed individuals with a demonstrated relevant expertise and experience, e.g., the social services arena, the educational spectrum, especially, *the 'voice' of the clients*, the juvenile and adult criminal justice systems, systems analysts, etc. and also selections from these panels, committees, study groups et al that address a particular aspect of the models of Sections VI and VII but do not include client representation. The first-hand voice of the 'clients' is a critically and unique inclusion to this process.

[6] Develop a **team-derived set of metrics** [and their data requirements], a policy for accountability for all pilot model activities [as a necessary prelude to a broader

area of application] and a pilot model assessment plan and time line including periodic reviews by individuals beyond the team membership.

[7] There is a reference in [5] to 'clients'; this term includes those living in and experiencing poverty as well as those individuals [within and beyond the family], agencies, support systems, advocates and groups providing daily services, support and interactions with 'clients'. It is critically important to include 'client representation' in the development of any site-specific pilot model and subsequent policy/programs. Not to do so will, inevitably, compromise the success of the pilot program.

[8] Relevant, meaningful and appropriate metrics are absolutely required for [a] site-specific pilot model development, [b] management of the pilot model program, [c] the identification of the pilot model dynamics, [d] pilot model performance assessment, [e] data requirements and data acquisition and, finally, [f] quantification of the accountability of pilot model program management performance.

Chapter X
Authors' Closing Commentary

Recent events, e.g., in Ferguson, Cleveland, Baltimore, etc., [R96], R97], [R98], [R99], [R100], have raised an abundance of questions about the 'cause and effect' of police policies, turmoil in the streets, loss of life, the obvious flaws in legal and justice systems and, really, so much more. The usual follow -- on efforts of all concerned or affected are to identify and punish -- however that may happen -- those responsible for the chaos that was apparently triggered by a single event.

The news media, police and civil authorities and a wide spectrum of local and not-so-local citizens and individuals, individually and collectively, did little to respond to these situations in a civil, humanitarian and responsible manner; conversely, their activities and behavior tended to add 'fuel to the responsive flames' of anger and discontent. These events usually have outcomes to [1] place the blame somewhere -- even anywhere -- and [2] offer a bevy of 'solutions' that were addressing 'symptoms' of a core cause of these sad and disruption-intensive scenarios. *{Authors' note: It may be helpful to recall [RB-1] that a 'systems view/perspective initially focuses upon the symptoms of a 'problematic situation' but, more importantly, it also looks beyond the always obvious 'symptoms' in order to identify and define the genesis[aka the 'core cause'] of the 'symptoms.' Dealing with 'symptoms,' historically, has been a choice of convenience as opposed to searching for the cause {aka the real or core problem} of the symptoms. Fixing 'symptoms' -- whether it be social issues, education,* *engineering, et al always seems to be attractive to many but, in truth, 'fixing' symptoms can never provide a lasting response to the real or core problem.]* Attorney General Loretta Lynch [R101] advocates 'a national dialogue and other immediate necessities about race relations, law enforcement, social issues et al.' Certainly, this [continuing] dialogue is a necessity but it is one important 'piece' of a systemic 'problem' that requires a systemic solution; it may well represent a step in the proper direction. "Unfortunately, the problem of police interactions with blacks goes deeper than that. It goes to jobs, poverty, the justice system and opportunity. It also goes to a long history of mistrust, fear, and stereotyping from those unable to engage in real dialogue." History has also demonstrated that there is a time for great events...perhaps, just perhaps, this is a beginning. Only time will tell!

What, then, is the core cause?

History has long provided a 'voice' for those who have been relegated to a life of poverty of opportunity, economics, choice, 'voice', mistrust, fear and more.......*through no fault of their own.* It bears repeating that the aggregate impact of these inequalities is, clearly and undeniably, *unfair, undeserved, unnecessary and unacceptable.* The available literature for well over a century provides a rich-and steadily growing-reservoir of documentation and 'voices' that confirm these four characterizations. Let's breathe some life, meaning and relevance to each of the four.

First, *'unfair'* certainly applies; should there be doubters or naysayers, let them think about what their lives would be like if they lived in this very unfair environment. Does the feeling of a growing and simmering anger come to mind? Each of us have felt anger in response to a single or several acts of unfairness during our respective lives. Then, think about the preponderance of unfairness for those in multiple measures of poverty for extended durations of lengths of time: year after year after year... and decade after decade after decade.

A riot is the language of the unheard.

~Dr. Martin Luther King,
1966 interview with Mike Wallace

Secondly, *'undeserved'* is equally applicable and, in reality, is a multiplying factor for the long simmering anger innate within an unfair situation.

Thirdly, *'unnecessary'* is an interesting descriptor and becomes even a very shameful one given the untested and untried systemic plans, policies and programs rather than those addressing 'pieces' and 'symptoms' so engrained in an *'unfair, undeserved and unnecessary'* situation.

Finally, *'unacceptable'* is absolutely applicable when one considers the aggregate of costs not only of dollars and time but, of equal or greater importance, are the costs in opportunity, individually and nationally, quality of life and, yes, humanity. Acknowledgement of something, anything that is unacceptable *should and could* be the impetus to "do something about it!"

Returning to 'history' and its meaning and messages; First and foremost, the Constitution of the United States certainly qualifies as the initial, most dominant, well-known, persuasive and foundational national 'voice' for equality and fairness for all...not just some! A still growing array: William Wilberforce, an early abolitionist and advocate of human conditions and rights, [R2], Abraham Lincoln, W.E.B. Dubois, Dr. Martin Luther King, John F. Kennedy, Hubert Humphrey, civil right activists and advocates ...and, more recently, Ronald Kuykendall.

Social Crisis and Social Demoralization **by Ronald Kuykendall [R102]** offers that race relations, i.e., racial antagonism, racial antipathy and racial inequality within the United States is a continuing 'problem'...the authors themselves feel -- and have so written -- that it has been a continuing 'problem' for too long of a time. Additionally,

106

Kuykendall offers that [national, state and local] responses have addressed' symptoms of the African American condition and *"symptoms are not causes."* He also states "...the treatment of symptoms cannot cure [although it may alleviate] the discomfort." [R103] is an interesting interview of Ronald Kuykendall by Kam Williams. The questions posed to Williams are both direct and indirect, relevant and irrelevant; One of Kuykendall's response to one question is that...."therapeutic intervention is necessary to begin addressing the *many problems* within the ghetto." This statement is another experienced perspective that poverty-driven situations are, indeed, multidimensional and a subliminal message that a systemic methodology needs to be put in place.

Another question submitted during the interview by Williams referred to Kuykendall's book as, perhaps, an update of W.E.B. Dubois' *Talented Tenth Theory* [105]. W.E.B. Dubois, born in Massachusetts in 1868 and initially educated at Fisk University in Tennessee as a young teen; this education was complemented as he received a real-world education in racism, poverty, prejudices. He furthered his education at Harvard University and was awarded his doctorate in 1891[104]. A companion reference [106] cites excerpts from 105 and is equally informative and enlightening.

In September of 1903, Dubois wrote *The Talented Tenth* published in *The Negro Problem*. This article is an enlightening document from the post-Civil War days and is one of the earliest calls that 'something must be done!' This prejudice, racism and, yes, *unfairness* still remains part of the American culture and landscape. Interestingly enough, Dubois mentions the concept of lifting African-Americans up, that education and work [employment] are the uplifting keys as is the role of ideals in education and work. Returning to the events of Ferguson, Cleveland, Baltimore, etc. and so many less known similar events over a number of decades, a good question is *"What lies in the future?"* It seems quite likely that the recent -- and utterly tragic -- event at the Emanuel African Methodist Episcopal church may just be the 'tip of the iceberg' and fueled by anger, racism and misguidance of epic proportions [R107]. Taylor's comments on the NBC Evening

News on June 19, 2015 indicated that this shooting was an [inevitable] outcome of a deeply imbedded culture and its long, very long simmering 'pot' of hate, racism, prejudice and anger. This observation was provided by Paul C. Taylor, Associate Professor of Philosophy and African American Studies at Penn State University. He is also the author of *Race: A Philosophical Introduction* [R108]. This latter book is especially for those students and scholars in ethnic studies, philosophy and, especially, sociology.

A recently waved 'red flag' is "Riots, anger could erupt here," [R109], by Ray Hull, a State Representative from Providence, RI and a Sergeant in the Providence Police Department. His comments begin with the responsibility of police to 'protect all members of the community'; a principle engrained in the United States Constitution which, as the authors have said -- and written -- more than a few times, is applicable to all citizens: not just some of them but, indeed, all of them. Some reflection upon those recent riots and disturbance in the inner cities indicates quite emphatically that this 'responsibility to all' becomes a mute entity. A more focused reflection upon the history of African-Americans in America reveals the same silence. However, and quite to the point, history has abundantly demonstrated that this simply isn't true for those who survive in an *unfair, undeserved, unnecessary and unacceptable situation.* Hull also points out: *"Because of what happened in Baltimore, and what is happening in cities across the country, could happen here."* Hull also offers a snapshot of such a situation in Providence...the authors of this book would add "and elsewhere" to his statement.

However, there is another side to the recent tragedy in Charleston, South Carolina. On June 29, 2015, a Providence Journal *Commentary* entitled *Amazing Grace* [R110] was/is so relevant that the authors chose to include it in its entirety rather than a summary or selected excerpts. It follows:

AMAZING GRACE

If a young white man hoped to ignite a racial war with his al-leged slaughter of nine blacks at a historic church in South Carolina, he failed miserably.

The horrifying incident seems to have brought out the best in people. People of all races and backgrounds have joined together in mourning the loss, comforting the afflicted and expressing solidarity against violence.

But perhaps the most remarkable response has been from fam-ily members, expressing love and forgiveness rather than hatred and a desire for vengeance.

In our modern world of instant communications via social me-dia, the dominant message often seems to be incessant self-righteous-ness. Often this is accompanied by a desire to crudely insult and pun-ish those who disagree.

In this climate, tragedies can become instant fodder for scor-ing political points, taking the focus off of those whose lives have been shattered. It is easy to get the impression from Twitter and Facebook that hatreds rule our society, and nasty people make up the majority, given the hair-trigger vilification always at the ready.

But the people of Charleston have shown there is another America. They did not respond to the savage attack on their commu-nity with riots and rage but with sorrow, humility and a desire to change the world for the better through love of their fellow human beings. This remarkable spirit seems to reflect the best of their reli-gious faith.

Many fond of praising Abraham Lincoln seem to forget his Second Inaugural Address, as the blood-bath of the Civil War neared its end, he did not heed the North's understandable desire for venge-ance against the Confederacy but advocated healing. Admitting that he could only guess God's will, he called for "malice toward none" and "charity for all," and urged all Americans to "bind up the nation's wounds, to care for him who shall have borne the battle and for his widow and his orphan, to do all which may achieve and cherish a just and lasting peace among ourselves and will all nations."

The response of family members-love, not hatred-is a renewed challenge to all Americans to seek a just and lasting peace. In our view, we have a mighty task before us in striving to honor this nation's noble ideals. It would help to converse with each other in a spirit of charity, not malice.

***

It is remarkable -- even ironic -- that despite those many 'voices' that have, over so many decades, called for 'freedom for all', it is the collective 'voice' of members of a long-oppressed community who have 'showed America the way'!

Another local touch of irony is that *Let's Start with the Children* [R2] cites a 15 year ministry in the South Bronx that was inspired by *Amazing Grace* [R111] and fueled by the spiritual hymn, Amazing Grace, and its message and meaning!

A more direct message, *America-What Do We Do After Charleston?* [R112], provides a very reality-based, compassionate, compelling and hopeful message for the future!

More emphatically, the [almost] inevitable outcomes [R113] of these *unfair, undeserved, unnecessary and unacceptable situations* will likely mean more -- and not just a few -- similar tragedies in the coming years.......*unless we, the citizenry of America, all of America, breathe life, commitment, leadership and American ideals and principals into those long overdue efforts that will forever silence the anguished cries of so many for so long, i.e., that "Something must be done!"*

Angus Deaton, an economist at Princeton University, was awarded the Nobel prize for his work in the field of economics. Prior to that award, Professor Deaton worked on 'issues of poverty and inequality long before the financial crisis made them voguish.' A recommended article [R115] is well worth reading.

A quotation by George Bernard Shaw [R114], paraphrased by Robert F. Kennedy in his 1968 presidential campaign, used by John F. Kennedy and offered by Senator Ted Kennedy in his eulogy speaking of his brother, Robert F. Kennedy:

"Some see things as they are and ask 'Why?' ...some see things as they could be and ask 'Why not?'

'If not now, when?'"

Chapter XI
Appendices

APPENDIX A: 'Systems' Prologue

Just what do 'system', 'systemic', 'systematic', 'systems perspective', 'systems lens', 'systems analysis' really mean beyond the words? Since this book emphatically advocates the need for 'a comprehensive, meaningful, high-utility and relevant *systems perspective*' as others [e.g., R16, R21] have also inferred, stated and concluded that the inner city poverty and educational situation is, indeed, *systemic*, it is critically necessary to understand some *systems principles and practices*. Simply put, one needs to acquire a 'systems mindset'. Such an understanding comes in two very distinct phases: first, a recognition that the inner city poverty and educational arena et al is very much a system -- actually, an entity of many subsystems and can be *functionally* modeled as such; secondly, understand that this functional definition allows the application of firmly established *systems engineering and analysis methodologies* [RA-1].

Initially, there will be the inevitable 'doubt' and 'reluctance' on the part of some of the readers to acknowledge and embrace 'the systems engineering approach to model the inner city poverty and educational' linkage. Again, the key is to 'see' that the inner city poverty and educational arena is very much a 'system'! Let us review some of the principles provided by Kossiakoff et al [RA-2]:

- "The function of systems engineering is to *guide the engineering of complex systems.*" 'Engineering' is **"the application of scientific principles to practical ends."** Simply put 'engineering' is that process employed to have a 'system' -- *any system, especially a complex system* -- do what it should be doing.

- **"....a system is a** "set of interrelated components **working** together toward some *common* objective." The authors respectfully submit that a system's components, i.e., subfunctions, *should* be working together. However, there are 'systems' that simply do not work well toward some common objectives [s] for a variety of reasons, e.g., lack of resources, ineffective and/or inefficient management, insufficient understanding of 'what's going on', erroneous or unsubstantiated requirements, innate system complexity, external [to the system] disturbances and/or driving forces, etc.

- "This definition implies a multiplicity of interacting parts that commonly perform a significant function. The term *complex* restricts this above definition to systems in which the elements are diverse and have intricate relationships with one another." Collateral to the *complexity* of a system is its *nonlinear* characteristic [RA-3] that makes a system's projected performance quite difficult; the "good news," however, is that the availability of a wealth of relevant data could contribute to an inherent *adaptive capability* that could enable both system stability and improved performance.

- "Systems engineering is focused on the system as a whole." It also has the innate capacity to bring 'structure', 'order', 'understanding' and an inherent 'adaptive' capability [to counter unexpected and/or negative effects to performance] to a complex system. This process has the innate

113

advantage of enabling a focusing upon the problem rather than the symptoms of the problem. Dealing with the symptoms inevitably leads to temporary and ineffective 'fixes', aka 'band-aid solutions' or 'addressing 'symptoms rather than core issues.'

- "It is concerned not only with the [engineering] design of the system but also, a priori, an awareness of those external factors which can significantly constrain the design and, and, therefore, the level of performance."

- Speaking about 'system engineers': "...responsible for the formative (concept development) stage of a new system development, which culminates the functional design of the system *reflecting the needs of the user.*" It is vitally important that the 'system users' and their needs have a 'voice' in the formulation of modifications to what, in great part, is a 'broken system'. Historically, the omission of the users' perspective inevitably introduces significant risk to the cost, performance and useful system life.

Do the above six points convey some relevance to the inner city poverty and education et al situation? Do these six points convey the message that a *systems perspective* is an absolute necessity in order to 'shape' the outcomes of a specific and very complex system?

What is a 'system', then? It is an entity -- a function [1] -- with outcomes [2] that are the system's response to a set of requirements [3] via a set of sub-functions, i.e., derivatives of [1], which interact, dynamically, with each other to yield outcomes. Each 'system' is continuously managed with regard to performance requirements [4], assisted by 'feedback' [7], i.e., 'what's going on along a timeline', available resources [6] all based upon a diligent and responsible use of resource-dependent strategies [5]. This definition of a 'system' is provided in its canonical form in Figure 1.

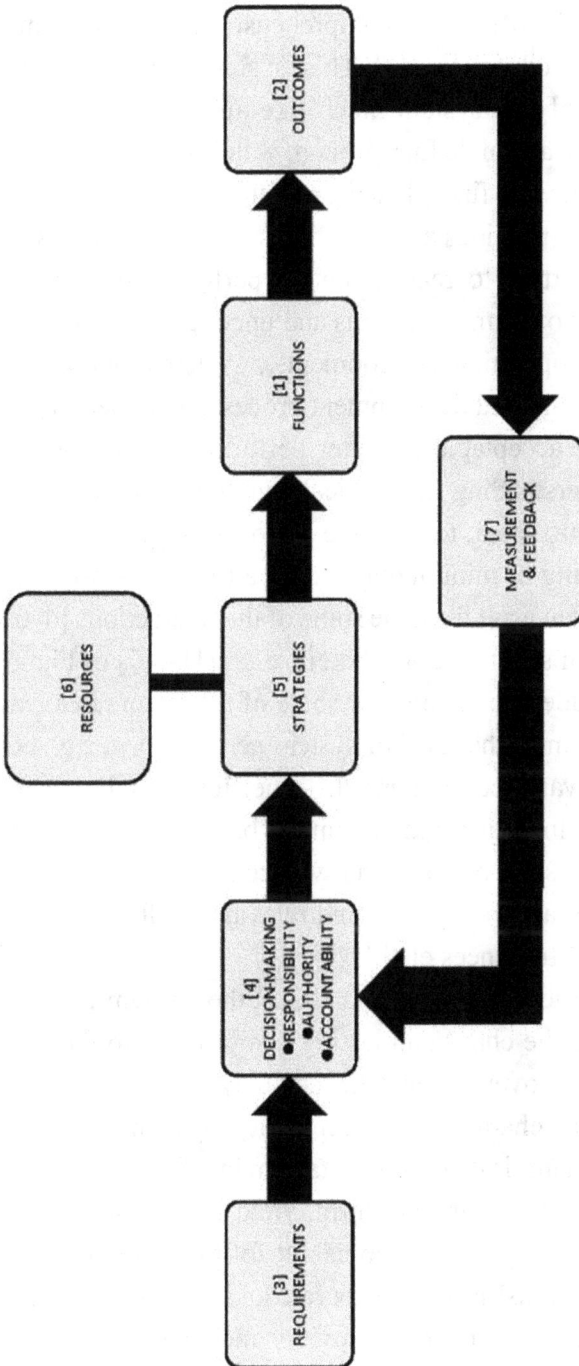

FIGURE 1 - CANONICAL FORM/MODEL FOR ANY SYSTEM

This system arrangement is the core or building block for *any system* and is used to develop a comprehensive and credible model of inner city poverty, education et al. This 'system' is a *functional* representation/model of any system much like an organization, a school system, a website, a vehicle [air, ground, water, space], industry, agriculture, health, etc. At first glance, the set of these basic functional components really provides a top-level description of *any system!*

It is important to realize that a 'perfect system' rarely exists…each has its own imperfections and uncertainties within the system, per se, and operating environment… systems that are well ordered [via the design and development process] and operationally understood provide acceptable or better performance [outcomes]. This 'order' and 'understanding' are critical enabling factors so necessary and, hopefully, sufficient, to improve performance… usually by continually eliminating or minimizing -- over a timeline -- the inevitable 'imperfections' that arise from the some of the interactions [dynamics] amongst the set of sub-functions therein, e.g., [1] – [7] of Figure 1.

Just an added note; consider some of the factors that may very seriously compromise the level of system performance, e.g., conflicting and/or irrelevant requirements [3], inefficient and/or ineffective management [4], initiation and pursuit of 'band-aid solutions. [5], insufficient resources [6], a lack of knowledge of 'what's going on' [aka lack of sufficient, accurate timely and relevant feedback [7], external [to the system] disturbances et al.

Also, consider how each and all, i.e. the 'system', of these factors contribute to the chaos and lasting compromise to the quality of life in the areas of poverty wherever they may exist.

The unique character of an inner city 'system' or any poverty stricken area 'system' is that each contain an innate set of [debilitating] imperfections that, in aggregate form, yield *unfair, undeserved, unnecessary* and *unacceptable* outcomes. It follows directly that candidate 'system solutions' must incorporate and address this 'aggregate form'. The forthcoming inner city poverty and educational models are intended to give meaning and clarity to this discussion.

Finally, Webster tells us that a 'system' is a set or arrangement of things as related or connected as to form a unity or organic whole. Webster offers another interesting definition: 'the body considered as a functioning organism'. Could we then call any poverty-stricken area as an organic whole, a functioning organism that yields a wide spectrum of outcomes too many of which are undesirable or, more to the point, *unfair, undeserved, unnecessary and unacceptable* leading to the degradation of the overall quality of life of millions of residents-in-poverty, their humanity and their exclusion from those opportunities readily available to those beyond the inner cities? The enormous cost in $$ expended on 'system' maintenance rather than marked and durable 'system' improvement only serves to exacerbate the situation!

Appendix A References

RA-1 Systems Engineering and Analysis, Benjamin A. Blanchard, Wolter J. Fabrycky, Prentice Hall, February 6, 2010.

RA-2 Systems Engineering Principles and Practices, Second Edition, Alexander Kossiakoff, William N. Sweet, Samuel J. Seymour, Steven M. Biemer, John Wiley & Sons, New York, 2011.

RA-3 Design Criteria and Algorithms for Adaptive Control Systems, A Thesis Submitted in Partial Fulfillment of the Requirements for the Degree of Philosophy in Electrical Engineering, Albert M. Colella, University of Rhode Island, 1973.

APPENDIX B: Model Hierarchy Granularity, Utility and Scalability

Whereas the 'poverty' and 'education' models provided in Sections V, VI and VII [the 'what are they'], this section addresses [1] the [vertical and horizontal *'hierarchy'* of the model, its *'granularity'*. [3] its *'scalability'* and [4] the potential *'utility'* of the models on a local, state and/or national application. Also, what is needed to make the models 'work', i.e., be meaningful for the *identification, development, time-based assessment and modification* of plans, policies and strategies. This model-like all models -- is a 'living' entity and requires updating as some model components are determined to be valid and relevant while others become irrelevant with the passage of time and the inevitable changing operational environment.

Emphasis is also focused upon the real-time likely required for the models to yield real-world feasibility via relevant, credible and quantitative measures of performance, aka *'metrics'*. For the systems with an innate complexity such as those identified and discussed in Sections VI and VII, the authors' expectations are firmly grounded in an extended timeline of years and, perhaps, decades for improvement, i.e., the continuing minimization and/or elimination of long-standing inequalities. There will be no quick answers or solutions. Let us understand that there is a very formidable amount of *inertia* within the spectrum of functions addressed in Sections VI and VII. This entity of *inertia* inevitably manifests itself as a deterrent to change and progress. This entity is really a tendency [for a variety of reasons] to remain in the status quo without change; it is really a reluctance [for whatever reason] to move; it is a lack of desire; it is an act of turning away in the face of reality and the overwhelming requirement to, in fact, move forward. Placing a priority upon change is, without question, the right thing to do, the humanitarian thing to do, the American thing to do!

This *'social inertia'* has many ingredients: racism, the spectrum of inequalities, imbedded cultural practices and protocols, priorities gone astray, blindness to humanity, lack of leadership, a misguided system of values, lack of accountability, lack of acknowledgement for the human, dollar and opportunity costs, social complacency et al. Each of these is addressed within this document, e.g., Section III entitled *Why?* The point being made here is it will take time, resources, national leadership and, especially, a lasting commitment to overcome this long-imbedded social inertia. Simply put, this form of inertia is the lack of movement or activity especially when movement is needed and/or wanted {Merriam-Webster dictionary}. However, there is a positive version of inertia; essentially, that a system in motion will stay in motion until opposing forces are brought to bear. Can we infer, then, that the task before America is to transition from the former [the status quo] to the latter [social and humanitarian progress, aka a 'level playing field' for all]?

Some Necessary Context

The poverty and education models of text Figures 2, 3, 4 and 5 [Section V] are stepping stones to the definition of the duality of a functional hierarchy and its linkage to its partner, i.e., performance hierarchy. In a 1973 publication [RA-1] there was a projection that the process of simulation so widely used so successfully in space, military, logistical, medical, business and flow applications would inevitably be extended to socio-economic situations. The passage of time has certainly validated this projection. Figure 1.1 of [RA-1] is provided on the following page. This figure is an example of the functional definition of the process of 'system simulation' that provides a systems insight, understanding et al *with minimum risk of dollars and time*; it portrays *'what* the system is doing and *how well* it is being done' --

the latter [via 'metrics'] is a critical necessity for a credible extrapolation of the model performance to a real-world environment. This reference

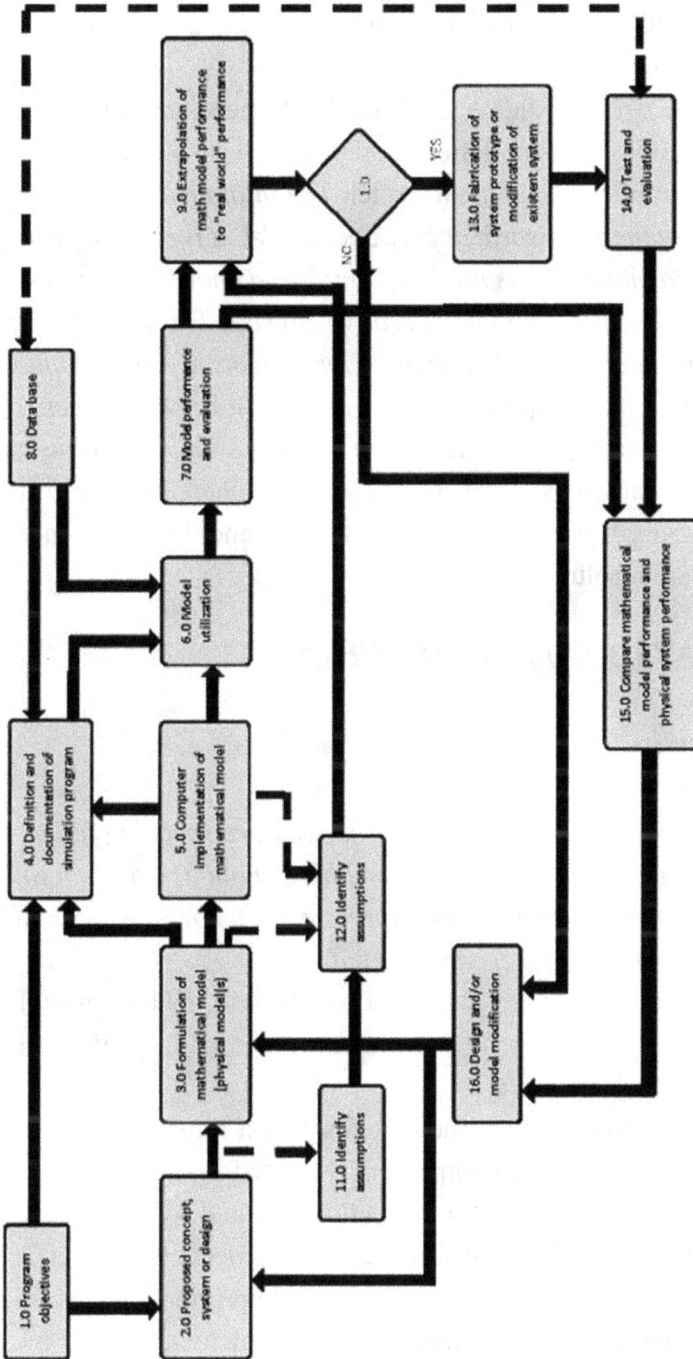

FIGURE B-1 - THE PROCESS OF SIMULATION FROM [RB-1]

also addresses the criteria for the process of simulation when the complexity and convolution of a system *preclude a mathematical formulation and solution.*

A very candidate [and inevitably necessary alternative] is to use some type of simulation model, e.g., a prototype, pilot, scale or even a simplified analytical model. *The pilot model is an operational version of the real-world operational model. It is really a prototype/pilot hybrid model that is used to identify and understand system dynamics while incurring minimum real-world risk. This hybrid model is especially necessary and applicable for systems of high complexity with its network of network of linkages and the acknowledgement of a lack of understanding of the interaction between system functions and these linkages and, most importantly, their impact upon system performance. Simply put, this* hybrid model is a candidate platform to enable total system solutions.

THE NECESSITY of METRICS

Preamble

When you can measure what you are speaking about, and express it in numbers, you know something about it; but when you cannot measure it, when you cannot express it in numbers, your knowledge is of a meager and unsatisfactory kind.

~**Lord Kelvin**, 19th Century Physicist
[Reference [RB-7]

Imbedded within the systems of text Figures 2, 3, 4 and 5 [and especially those more comprehensive user-friendly website [*Poverty-Inequalities.com*] versions of Sections VI and VII] are the functions of on-line and off-line performance assessments and the efficient and effective use of these assessments to sustain/improve performance. In the real-world arena of operations, this statement simply means that there is a need for 'metrics'. These 'metrics' must be relevant, credible, accurate, timely and meaningful for all concerned parties: those with system management and accountability responsibilities, the administrators, operational personnel, budgeteers et al but, most of all, for the spectrum of clients to be served by the system! Let us not forget the words of Abraham Lincoln: "Government of the people, by the people and *for the people.*" The important role of 'metrics' and the system network of linkages to all-levels of performance, authority, responsibility and accountability need to be addressed.

The innate necessity of metrics, meaningful metrics, in the online, real-time management of any system with the construct of Section V's Figures 1, 2, 3, 4 and 5 [as well as the versions of Sections VI and VII found at ***Poverty-Inequalities.com*** is directly obvious. An acceptable level of system performance cannot be achieved -- and sustained -- by the management of any given function without a reliable and timely knowledge of "What's working?" "What's not working?" "What's changing within the dynamics of this closed-loop system and its operational environment?" 'Dynamics' could manifest themselves in the near term but also in the [much] longer term of systems with imbedded and significant amounts of inertia, i.e., social inertia. This is especially applicable and necessary for systems of high-complexity and long term time-varying changes in operational conditions, e.g., the systems provided in the website models of Sections VI and VII. The role of metrics is also a critical necessity to have an 'adaptive' capability [aka, a plan B] imbedded into the system design. The more complex the system, the more variations within the system and its environment, the greater is the need for this 'adaptive' capability. This is one of the driving forces for the inclusion of 'metrics' in the models of Section VI and VII. The wealth of available literature of 'systems' research, design, implementation and operation reinforces the need for and the benefits of an 'adaptive' capability.

There are references in the available literature that do address various societal 'metrics' [aka measures of system performance] for those in both urban and rural poverty settings. For example, [RB-2] focuses upon the economy, job market, crime level and welfare of the population of *The Best and Worst Run Cities of America.* It is important to note that a single performance criterion, i.e., a set of metrics, 'doesn't fit all' because of significant variations from one city to another, one neighborhood to another, etc. This particular observation becomes increasingly critical when developing or shaping a plan, policy or program for a specific site.

Another important but subtle observation is the linkage between the 'function of city management' and the metrics employed including responsibility and accountability This reference also provides a website link to *The Ten Best-Run and Ten Worst-Run States in America.*

Another very interesting reference is *London: Contrasts In The Quality of Life Between the Inner City and the Suburbs* [RB-3]. This very informative and exemplary reference addresses the quality of life in the 32 boroughs of London [13 in 'inner' London and 19 in 'outer' London]. This 2004 government study/investigation focuses upon the national index of ' Multiple Deprivation'. This effort is quite analogous to the family 'indicators' [R59, R60] and is certainly reflective of the complexity and convolution of America's poverty areas.

The *Multiple Deprivation Index* includes seven areas of deprivation: income, employment, health deprivation and disability, education-skills training, barriers to housing and services, crime and disorder and the living environment. This very relevant reference also includes a methodology for quantifying six district measures of deprivation. This quantification allows an assessment of the most deprived boroughs across each of the district measures of deprivation.

The *2010 Charlotte Neighborhood Quality of Life* [RB-4] includes the premise of community leaders and urban analysts that the success of cities has critical linkage to vibrant, sustainable [a very important observation] neighborhoods. Twenty locally derived variables [again 'one size doesn't fit all'] are biennially addressed. This particular type of methodology for the measuring/quantifying the neighborhood-oriented quality of life is an integral component of the 'first step' toward tailoring/shaping plans/programs/policies for a specific site. Initially, this methodology is directly applicable to a 'pilot program' and its assessment within the process of determining the feasibility of a candidate/proposed program or policy.

Similar quality of life studies have been done for Oklahoma City [RB-5] and Kansas City [RB-6]. These two 2010 studies develop a numerical scale for ten indices and compare these results to those of their respective states as well as a reference level of 100 for the United States.

These five representative studies provide a context for the effort required to quantify [as best as possible] via a set of site specific performance criteria, i.e., a set of metrics. Simply put, the metrics provide the foundation for the tracking/monitoring an improving, declining or an unchanging quality of life. The 'quality of life' is reflected within the spectrum of outcomes in the poverty and education models of Sections VI and VII, respectively.

It is important to note that, although the spectrum of outcome metrics has widely varying ranges of values, the methodology exists to develop a single composite index for various and meaningful combinations of outcomes and their metrics including the inevitable weightings [priorities].

Some perspectives on 'system design'... the methodology/technology exists for the orderly design... or redesign/modification... of a complex [seemingly complicated and convoluted!] situation. In the latter, of course, there are more unknowns, uncertainties and limitations with which to cope. However, whether it is a design or redesign effort, the process of systems engineering addresses the bottom line of efficiency and effectiveness of both performance and cost for an extended length of time *in an orderly manner*. This process also includes the design-imbedded capacity to adapt to unforeseen events, circumstances et al. Additionally, this process integrates 'risk management' into the design [or redesign] process; it is not too difficult to perceive and understand the enormity of performance and budget risk without this latter consideration.

The option to the a priori process of systems analysis engineering principles is to continue with the a posteriori process of 'business as usual'!

Functional Hierarchy and Granularity

Figure B-2 provides the functional hierarchy of a well-ordered, well-defined system within a known operational environment. The top-level function [F0] is that same function identified within the canonical form of Figure 1, Figure 2 [Poverty] and Figure 3 [Educational Processes]. That top-level function is then defined in terms of each of the derivative functions: F1, F2, F3, ..., Fi; Then each of those level 2 functions, e.g., F3, are defined in terms of their derivative functions, e.g., F31, F32, F33, ..., F3m. That process leads to both a vertical functional hierarchy and an ever spreading horizontal hierarchy. The horizontal hierarchy enables the inclusion of relevant functions and the exclusion of those that are not...this process leads to the credibility of the overall model. The vertical hierarchy consistently leads to increasing levels of functional granularity.

Each function at every level has a dual performance entity; Figure B-3 provides the collateral performance hierarchy of a well-ordered, well-defined system. Relationships that functionally describe the functional and performance hierarchies are:

$$F_0 = f[F_1, F_2, F_3, ..., F_i]$$
$$F_3 = f[F_{31}, F_{32}, F_{33}, ..., F_{3m}]$$
$$F_{33} = f[F_{331}, F_{332}, F_{333}, ..., F_{33t}]$$

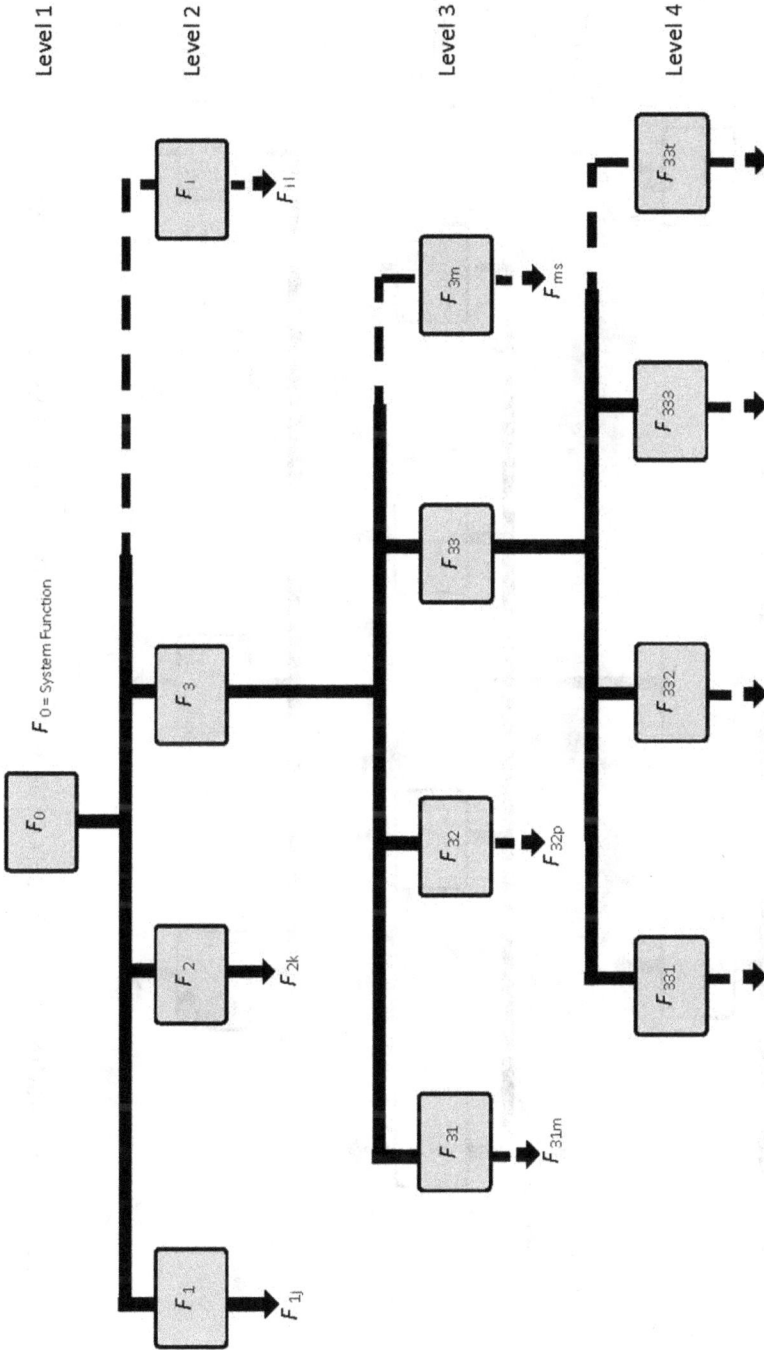

FIGURE B-2 - FUNCTIONAL HIERARCHY OF A 'WELL-ORDERED'…, 'WELL-DEFINED' SYSTEM

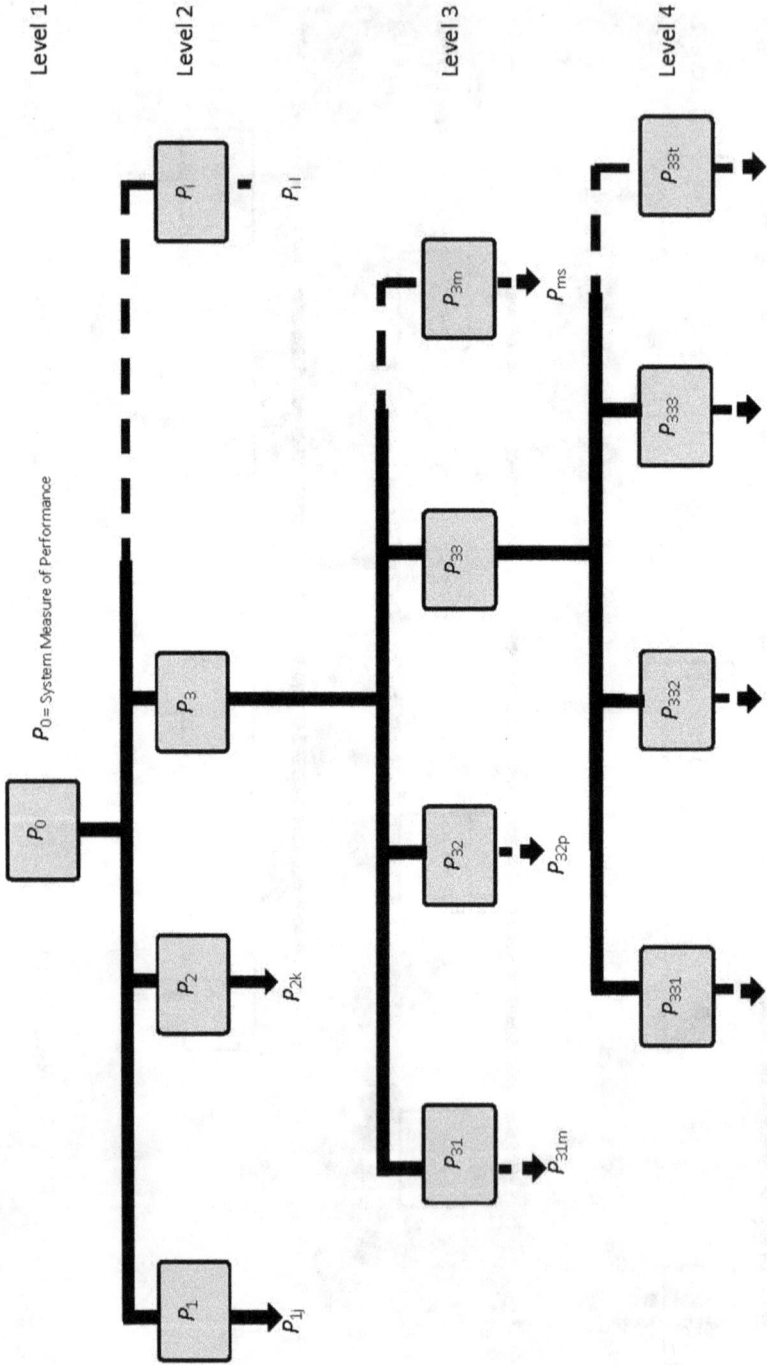

FIGURE B-3 - PERFORMANCE HIERARCHY OF A 'WELL-ORDERED'..., 'WELL-DEFINED' SYSTEM

Additional levels of performance granularity:

$$P_0 = f\,[P_1, P_2, P_3, ..., P_i]$$

$$P_1 = f\,[P_{31}, P_{32}, P_{33}, ..., P_{3m}]$$

$$P_{33} = f\,[P_{331}, P_{332}, P_{333}, ..., P_{33t}]$$

A word on the definition of a well-ordered and well-understood system: the systems of Figures B-2 and B-3 are so because each of the functional and performance levels are credible representations of the real-world systems. There is a minimum of uncertainty as well as a minimum of complexity due to 'linkages both known and unknown.'

The known 'linkages' are imbedded within the functional and performance hierarchies whereas the unknown 'linkages' are virtually non-existent. 'Order' and 'understanding' complement each other.

The point is that 'order' is the inevitable result of 'understanding': a point that is all-important for the development of a credible model. The 'model', in turn, offers the potential for an enhanced 'understanding', an enhanced 'order' and, of course, a greater level of a sustained system performance. This is the basic intent, motivation and message of this particular appendix.

Figures B-4 and B-5, from [RA-3], are examples of a well-ordered and well-understood Air Traffic Control [ATC] System. The ATC System top level 'measure of performance,' P00, is really a composite entity that reflects the aggregated performances enabled by the performance hierarchy of those function at the P1, P2 and P3 levels.

Compare the system structures of Figures B-2 to B-5 to the system structures of poverty and education addressed in Sections VI and VII and on the referenced website there. Specifically, the system structures of Figures B-4 and B-5 do not have the inherent characteristics of complexity, convolution and uncertainty of the poverty and

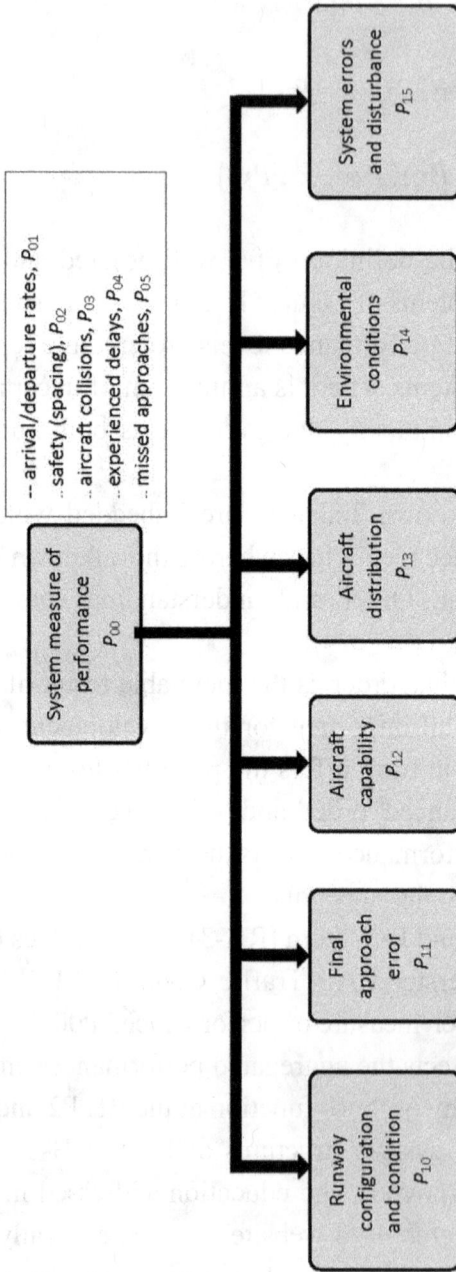

FIGURE B-4 - TOP LEVEL FUNCTIONAL ANALYSIS OF TERMINAL AREA AIR TRAFFIC CONTROL (ATC) SYSTEM (FROM [RB-1])

System measure of performance P_{00}

-- arrival/departure rates, P_{01}
.. safety (spacing), P_{02}
.. aircraft collisions, P_{03}
.. experienced delays, P_{04}
.. missed approaches, P_{05}

Runway configuration and condition P_{10}

Final approach error P_{11}

Aircraft capability P_{12}

Aircraft distribution P_{13}

Environmental conditions P_{14}

System errors and disturbance P_{15}

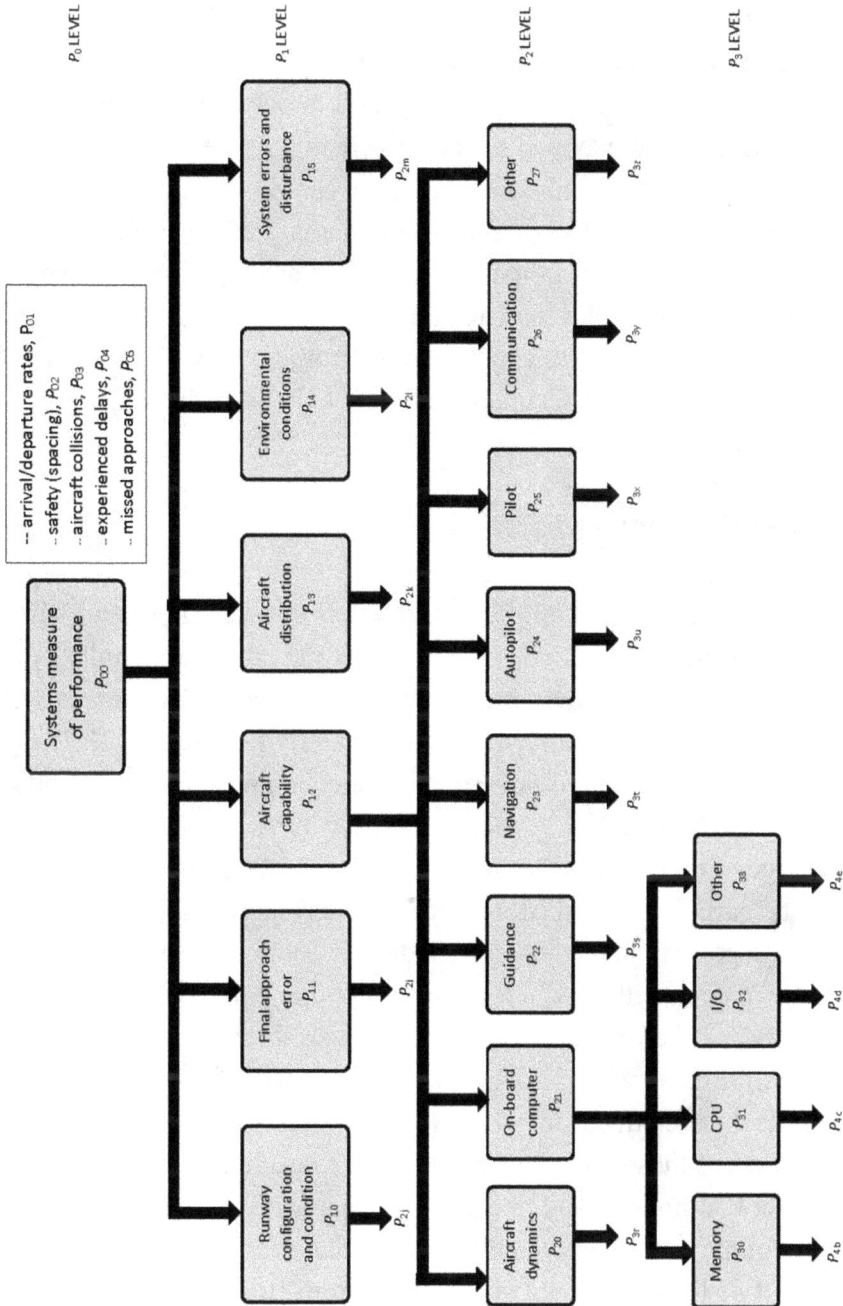

FIGURE B-5 - Total ATC SYSTEM STRUCTURE VIA FUNCTIONAL ANALYSIS (FROM RB-1)

education models with its imbedded network of 'linkages'. These 'linkages' pose an outstanding challenge to the development of candidate comprehensive solutions. The immediate difference is the apparent lack of order and understanding in the [initial] system structures for poverty and education. 'Understanding' and 'order' are prerequisites and a credible model may just be the vehicle to provide them.

A final note on 'linkages': 'linkages' can be expressed in analytical form, i.e., equations, graphics, data bases, statistical measures, +/- scales, text and/or functional descriptions. Each representation has its innate detail, accuracy and uncertainty. History has abundantly demonstrated that all credible system models migrate over time to increased detail, improved accuracy and the inevitable reduction/elimination of uncertainty.

Functional Utility and Scalability

First, the practical utility of the models of Sections VI and VII lies in the raising of the *'awareness'* level of the inherent complexity and convolution of the area of interest, i.e., the spectrum of inequalities that seem to persist within all areas of poverty [text Figure 2]. The representations [models] of poverty and education of Sections VI and VII -- both in their initial versions and their inevitable updates with the passage of time -- can provide a credible *'check-list'* for those who wish to be participants and contributors in the solution process.

The poverty and education models of Section VI and VII also offer the context within which to focus upon a 'part' or 'piece', i.e., *'scalability',* of the overall situation. However, there is, first, the requirement for those who choose to address a 'piece' of the problem to [1] include those elements they believe to be directly relevant but, also, [2] be aware of those elements they choose to exclude for reasons of convenience, simplicity and/or a focus upon a particular area of interest. Each of the excluded elements are candidates for assumptions, i.e., the impact of linkages is not significant. From [R62, page 20]: 'Re-

gardless of the proposed concept, system or design under consideration, there are always some relevant assumptions concerning system
operation or technological capability that must be eventually weighed
when attempting to extrapolate real world performance from the
model performance. These assumptions must be identified and, when-
ever possible, defined with respect to their effect upon real world performance... a strong effort must be made to determine the sensitivity
of the [extrapolation] prediction process to these assumptions.'

An acknowledgement of any exclusions from a 'partial model'
becomes a necessity in order to assess the real-world credibility of the
performance of the 'partial model' in light of these exclusions, i.e., assumptions.

The importance of *'order'* and *'understanding'* have been previously addressed.

The above considerations, each and all are related to the *'scalability'* process, i.e., a focus upon a specific site, neighborhood, town,
city or geographical area. This *'scalability'* is both necessary and feasible in order to develop and employ those *'metrics'* that need to be
shaped to a particular site, neighborhood, town, city or geographical
area, e.g., [RB-3]. This 'shaping' of metrics must include individuals
from the particular area of interest: administrators, managers, relevant
experienced professional and, especially area clients who always seem
to lack representation. These considerations are, of course, prerequisites to the solution process! As mentioned previously, an obvious
metric for planning, program and policy success, in time, will be a
simplification of this representation/model as the spectrum of inequality outcomes is reduced/eliminated.

Appendix B References

RB-1: Systems Simulation: Methods and Applications, A.M. Colella, M.J.
O'Sullivan, D. J. Carlino, Lexington Books, Lexington, MA, 1974.

RB-2: The Best and Worst Run Cities of America, Mike Sauter, http://247/wallst.com, January 2, 2014

RB-3: London: Contrasts In the Quality of Life Between the Inner City and the Suburbs, Human Geography, http://geocases2.co.uk/londonsuburbs1.htm, August 19, 2012.

RB-4 2010 Charlotte Neighborhood Quality of Life Study, The Challenge and Good News, http://ui.uncc.edu/story/2010.

Rb-5 Oklahoma City, OK 73159 Quality of Life Indexes, clrsearch.com, 2010.

RB-6: Kansas City, MO 64127 Quality of Life Indexes, clrsearch.com, 2010.

RB-7: A Short History of the Revolving Door, William E. Colleran, OP-ED Contributor, Providence Journal, April 24, 1992.

APPENDIX C: Life Cycle Costs-What are they? A necessary part of the solution?

This section addresses the definition of life cycle costing and its relevance as an integral part of the comprehensive solution to re-duce/eliminate the inequities associated with the real-world outcomes of the models of Sections VI and VII.

What Is Life Cycle Costing?

Life Cycle Costing [LCC] is a process/methodology that, ini-tially, was employed to determine the minimum cost alternatives for a 'system' to be considered for design, development, testing & evalua-tion, implementation, maintenance and support throughout the ex-pected life of the 'system'. LCC also includes, when applicable, those costs of removing the 'system' from the operational arena and its sub-sequent disposal. Simply put, the 'true cost' of a system is not is not just the initial costs associated with putting the system into service but rather the aggregated costs over the life of the system. The former costs, historically, are an unexpectedly and a relatively smaller cost as compared to the life cycle costs [RC-1].

1.8 Life Cycle Costing [RC-2] provides a more formal defini-tion: 'Life cycle Costing [LCC] is an important economic analysis used in the selection of the least cost alternatives for a twenty year period'. 'Cost' has been, historically, measured in USD! This particular refer-ence also provides a procedural summary and description of the LCC methodology. This LCC methodology has gained increasingly wide-spread application by both the Federal government and corporate America for the past three or four decades. If one were to do a WWW search for LCC Analysis, the resultant number of 'hits' would exceed 50,000,000; this represents not only a formidable acceptance of LCC but also a reservoir of 'mining opportunities' for LCC references and documentation. It is a quiet and subtle -- but uniquely important -- note that the level of performance must be a common thread within each of the least cost alternatives. The LCC methodology offers the quantification of the ultimate measure of system performance and cost, i.e., the sensitivity of performance measures [metrics] to total costs; simply put, the 'biggest bang for the buck'!

For the many applications in manufacturing, technology, military systems, transportation, construction et al, the list of costs for each of the applications has become well established over the last few decades. These costs can be deterministic [known with a high degree of certainty] or statistical [known with varying -- but significant-- levels of uncertainty]. It suffices to say that there is a direct linkage between uncertainty and risk. In fact, *risk management* addresses *uncertainty.* A complete life cycle cost projection [LCCP] analysis may include related costs, e.g., interest rates, depreciation, present value of money/discount rates and other costs that reflect relevant and necessary *and unnecessary* expenditures [RC-3]. One of the more comprehensive treatments of LCC is the Mitre Corporation's Systems Engineering Guide [RC-4].

LCC Relevance to a Solution to the Inequalities Spectrum

First and foremost is the acknowledgement that the often mentioned spectrum of inequalities was forged over years and decades... *and...* was essentially 'maintained' during that time despite the many commendable efforts to reduce/eliminate those inequalities. Let the naysayers and procrastinators, i.e., those who are too willing to 'kick the can down the road', offer their weak rationale that 'we have done this, we have done that, etc., etc. etc.', keep in mind that the inequalities to a great degree still remain *unfair, undeserved, unnecessary and unacceptable!* Let all Americans recognize that what took years to create will not be solved quickly; any solution will be a long-term process. *The development, implementation, on-going assessment and realization of a sustainable, meaningful, endurable and cost-effective solution will be a long-term process.* Any solution <u>*must*</u> be sustainable, meaningful, enduring and cost-effective. *The true costs of any solution must include not only dollar costs but also the costs in opportunities and the quality of life [as currently reflected in the spectrum of inequalities]!* For systems of high complexity and convolution, total cost needs to include both those easily identifiable USD costs but also costs linked to more intangible entities, e.g., loss of opportunities, racism, quality of life, etc.

Finally, there is a required common thread through [a] the life and dynamics, i.e., variations as a function of time, of the long history of the development and maintenance of the current status quo situation, [b] that time and those dynamics of a 'solution', i.e., a reversal of the status quo as measured by the sustained decrease in the spectrum of inequities and, of course, the required time for a necessary, sufficient and cost-effective budgeting process.

It is important to recognize that most annual budgeting processes addressing the spectrum of inequalities usually exclude the impact of the many 'linkages' to areas beyond that of a particular budget. *It is the impact of these linkages that lead to a shortened life for the expected benefits as well as a significant compromise in the intended effectiveness and efficiency 'promised' by this particular budget.*

Considering the long, long, l-o-n-g time consumed for the development and maintenance of the status quo, the expected time duration likely required for the maturity of a solution process and, finally, the time required -- and committed -- to a necessary and sufficient long-term cost-effective budgeting process, there are two indicators of total cost over a sustained period of time, i.e., the time required for a solution process to yield a measurable, sustainable, meaningful [with regard to humanity], endurable and cost-effective, i.e., [performance/dollar, aka 'the biggest bang for the buck'] outcome. Once again, there will be no quick solutions; it will take years -- maybe decades -- to overcome the well-imbedded *social and political inertia.*

First, there is the total cost [TC] of maintaining the status quo [SQ] -- call it [TC/SQ] -- and its collateral spectrum of inequalities.

This total cost is not just the addition of those dollars expended annually for programs of aid and assistance but also for those dollars expended due to the costs of 'treating' -- but also 'maintaining' the same spectrum of inequalities year after year after year...... expenditures for medical assistance, housing, poverty-driven costs, educational-disadvantage-costs, unemployment costs, crime-related costs, costs of violence and social disorder, justice system costs, incarceration, costs, recidivism costs, et al. The aggregation of these costs can be determined for a period of time, e.g., fifteen or twenty years: the total costs could be referred to as the life cycle costs for the status quo for this particular period of time. *It is important to note that there would, probably, not be a significant lateral reduction and/or elimination in the spectrum of inequities. History certainly supports this inference, e.g., [R59, R76]. For example, the naysayers and the short-term advocates can still claim that the poverty rate of children in 2013 dropped by 1.9%. The realists could ask "True! But what about the remaining 19.9%?" The current spectrum of inequalities still exacts an immeasurable cost in dollars, opportunities, the quality of life and humanity!* The continuing persistence of the **spectrum of inequalities is driven by the** exclusion of the real-world impact of the network of linkages supported by a lack of a long-term, real-world oriented, humanitarian and systemic perspective.

Secondly, there is an option -- an opportunity actually -- to integrate LCC analysis into the initial and continuing planning, development, continuing assessment and updating of the solution process that *would cost significantly less dollars and, at the same time, reduce and/or eliminate the horrendous and costly impact of the many inequities.*

Let's take an example that can be duplicated across any and all of the poverty, disadvantaged and disenfranchised populations. Consider an individual who becomes a product of his/her environment starting at birth and continuing for his/her lifetime. This individual -- one of many millions -- is so often shaped by the impact of poverty: lack of family stability, a poor or even non-existent education at best, poor health, lack of a nurturing arena, lack of opportunity, lack of life skills, lack of advocacy, lack of effective legal counsel and representation, imbedded racism, ...and so much more.

This individual represents -- through no fault of his/her own -- a continuing drain on local and national resources. The treatment of this legacy of poverty over the lifetime of this individual consumes an inordinate amount of dollars, i.e., [TC/SQ]. If we aggregated the [TC/SQ] costs for all such individuals within a particular area, town, city, state or nation for a single year, we would be looking at the [TC/SQ] costs for a single year. A relevant note is that these disenfranchised and disadvantaged individuals are not contributing to society as so many Americans do...contributions not only in tax dollars, opportunities, quality of life and even those intangible gifts of creativity, artistry, technology et al. Imagine what the [TC/SQ] with an embarrassingly small 'return on investment' would be over ten, twenty or even a hundred years. Revisionist history is not an option but shaping the future certainly presents an attractive option ...'if and only if' conditions will be addressed in Section IX!

Conversely: with a systemic view [with an imbedded LCC analysis with total costs, [TC/LCC] over the coming years], would it be possible/feasible to provide budget, advocacy and support 'up-front' for some years to permanently reduce/eliminate some of the inequities driven by poverty and its 'linkages' to those other related factors depicted in Sections VI and VII? Although these 'up-front' costs would be, initially, substantial, would [TC/LCC] in an aggregated form across a neighborhood town, city, state or nation inevitably show a decrease once the status quo-enabled social and political inertia move in a constructive direction? Would the dynamics of the costs associated with inequities show a downward turn as the costs, [TC/SQ], via a [short-term] year-to-year budgeting view be overcome via 'up-front' investment that provides positive outcomes [sustainable, effective, enduring and cost-effective] and a continuing decrease in those traditional costs [TC/SQ] previously mentioned? In the former option, linkages are often excluded whereas these linkages become integral within a system-derived representation, e.g., those models in Sections VI and VII.

The initial question posed "What is the relevance of LLC analysis to a solution of the spectrum of inequalities?" Consider this: the total cost of the status quo [TC/SQ] -- however aggregated -- will be increasingly greater -- much greater -- than the latter option! Another way to say the same thing is that costs can be minimized via integrating LCC analysis in addressing the current situation with the collateral benefit that the 'returns on investment' will actually be added resources for America. Figure C-1 offers a comparative view of [TC/SQ], [TC/LCC] and their respective impact upon the spectrum of inequities and their respective 'intensities', potential savings and the availability of additional resources. [aka ROI on 'up-front' investments]. The comparative profiles of Figure C-1 are directly consistent with that array [more than 400] of 'life cycle costs curves available on the website entitled *Images for Life Cycle Costs Curves*.

Summarily, [TC/SQ] = the initial investment plus those annual costs to maintain, repair, update, modify a system, when aggregated over, say, a 10, 15 or 20 year period, may very well *significantly* exceed those 'true costs' [TC/LCC] incurred using models such as those provided in Sections VI and VII and LCC analysis over a 10, 15 or 20 year period. The current [TC/SQ] strategy and practice also yields an unnecessary and largely unproductive consumption of resources [dollars, time, personnel] simply to maintain the status quo.

The comparative profiles for [TC/SQ] and [TC/LCC] over a 20-year period reflect that [TC/SQ] costs have/are/will increase exponentially with [1] a collateral *decrease* in budget $$ for addressing the spectrum of inequities and, then, [2] an *increase* in the intensity of inequities and their impact upon the quality of life for those living in any of the poverty strata. Of the many very glaring examples of this intensity are the recent tragic and unfortunate events in Ferguson [Missouri], Cleveland, Baltimore et al. In the face of the extraordinary amount of media coverage, panels of experts, talk shows, social media

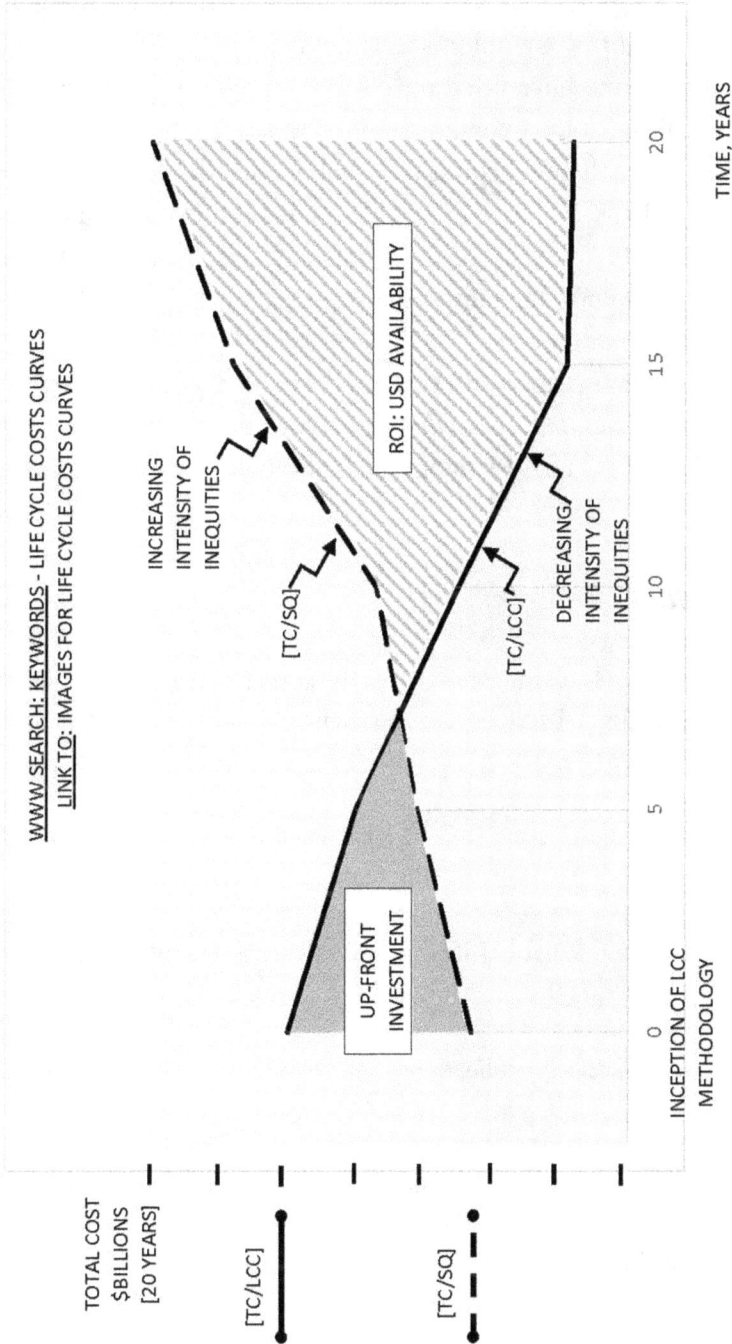

FIGURE C-1 - TOTAL [TC/SQ] AND [TC/LCC] PROFILES

chatter et al, there was little, if any, attention given to -- or interest in -- the *source/genesis* of the 'problem' rather than the apparent and alleged 'newsworthy' symptoms as candidate 'solutions' of the problem. Should someone have cried out *"Why?"*: a question that has already been put forth in the opening pages of this document. That's the 'bad news'! The 'good news' could very well be that the [TC/LCC] strategy will yield [1] an *increase* in available budget $$ and [2] a continuing *decrease* in the intensity of inequities and their historical and devastating impact upon humanity, their quality of life, opportunities, upward mobility and more.

At some point in time, then, the words of *unfair, undeserved, unnecessary and unacceptable* will no longer be applicable!

This [TC/LCC] strategy/methodology is an alternate strategy to [TC/SQ]!

Appendix C References

RC-1: Life Cycle Cost Models: Analysis and Methodology, Dr. A. M. Colella, 13th Joint Services Data Exchange for Initial Systems, St. Louis, MO, November 15, 1979.

RC-2: Life Cycle Costing [LCC], 2003 Facilities Standard, P100, 1.8 Life Cycle Costing, http://www.gsa.gov/portal/101197.

RC-3: Overview: What Is Life Cycle Costing?,simple.werf.org/Simple/media/LCCT/index.html.

RC-4: www.mitre.org/publications/system engineering guide/Systems Engineering Guide

RC-5: A Life Cycle Cost Summary, H. Paul Barringer, P.E., Barringer & Associates, Inc., International Conference of Maintenance Societies, ICOM-2003], May 23, 2003.

Chapter XII
Acknowledgements

As all authors and most people know, the efforts that lead to the publication of a book include the author's determination, passion, undaunted perseverance and self-confidence. However, the book's 'shape', message, content and publication are also fueled by the experiences of the author and the advocacy, support and encouragement of many individuals with whom he/she has shared his/her journey of life. ***Poverty & Despair vs. Education & Opportunity*** and its companion website, **Poverty-Inequalities.com**, is not an exception. There are more than a few individuals who have enabled and encouraged the recent efforts of the book's co-authors. Certainly friends, family and colleagues deserve acknowledgement for their constant support and advocacy -- and even their patience -- during the inevitable valleys of authorship.

However, the genesis and inspiration for this book lies with ***Let's Start with the Children*** and, in particular, the 'voices' of three individuals therein: Daniel Patrick Moynihan ["something must be done"], Dr. Martin Luther King ["we have come a long way but we still have a long, l-o-n-g way to go"] and James Patterson [author of ***Freedom Is Not Enough***].

Having said that, we would be remiss in our responsibilities as authors if we did not, specifically, cite the assistance, faith and encouragement of William Colleran, Grace Diaz, Ainsley Judge, Don Boucher, Pastor Janice Byers, PhD, A.T. Wall, Tricia Medeiros, Corporate Technology VP & Program Manager, the leadership of Frank Tweedie

[Dean, School of Engineering & Design at Johnson & Wales University], Jeffrey Tagen [Director, Innovation & Design Laboratory, School of Engineering & Design, JWU], Briana Ferraioli and Karissa Palmer, members of its Solution Team, Graphic Design Program. Particular acknowledgement is due to Dawn and Steven Porter of Stillwater River Publications for their consistent patience and contributions that enhanced the quality of the book.

These individuals-along with, literally, experiences and discussions with hundreds of students, teachers and educational administrators and researchers and, especially, residents within the arena of poverty -- made relevance, credibility and accuracy a necessary reality.

Finally, an enthusiastic note of gratitude and acknowledgement to my wife, Marion, who continuously provided the encouragement, time and space, love, patience and support that made my authorship possible. [*A.M.Colella*].

References

R1: Color Blind, Ellis Cose, Harper Perennial, 2001.

R2: Let's Start with the Children, Al Colella with Steven Lippincott, Westbow Press, 2013.

R3: Slave Ship, A Human History, Marcus Rediker, 2007.

R4: No Room at the Inn, Dr. Martin Luther King, Bennett College [900 E Washington St, Greensboro, NC], February, 11, 1958.

R5: Keep Slave History Alive [Ruth Simmons], Paul Davis, Education, Providence Journal, Journal, March 26, 2011.

R6: The Promised Land: The Great Migration and How It Changed America, Nicholas Lemann, Alfred A. Knopf, New York, 1991.

R7: The Warmth of Other Suns, Isabel Wilkerson, Random House, 2010.

R8: The Caging of America, Adam Gopnik, New Yorker Magazine, January 31, 2012.

R9: The Forgotten Man: A New History of the Great Depression, Amity Ahlaes, Harper Collins,2007.

R10: Black Like Me, Howard Griffin, Houghton Mifflin, Boston, 1961.

R11: To Be Equal, Charles Silberman, McGraw-Hill, New York, 1964.

R12: Shame of the Nation, Jonathan Kozol, Crown Publishers, 2005.

R13: Controversies of Poverty: Inequality, Income Growth and Mobility: The Basic Facts {Peter Gottschalk, Chapter Two, Changing Economy, It Takes a Nation: A New Agenda for Fighting Poverty [Rebecca Blank, Sandra Yu [as an MIT graduate student].

R14: Dark Ghetto: Dilemmas of Social Power, New Introduction by William Julius Wilson, Harper & Row, 1967.

R15: Freedom Is Not Enough, The Moynihan Report and America's Struggle over Black Family Life from LBJ to Obama, James T. Patterson, Basic books, Perseus Books Group, New York, 2010.

R16: The Negro Family: The case for National Action, {Daniel Patrick Moynihan}, Office of Policy Planning and Research, United States Department of Labor, March, 1965.

R17 Profiles In Courage, John F. Kennedy, Harper & Row, New York 1955, 1956, 1961.

R18: Horizons for Homeless Children, Boston, Massachusetts.

R19: What We Support, W. W. Kellogg Foundation, **http://www.wkkf.org**

R20: The Moynihan Report [R16] Revisited: Lessons and Reflections After Four decades, Harvard University Conference, 2007, Sage Publications, Thousand Oaks, California, 2009.

R21: So Rich, So Poor, Peter Edelman, The New Press, New York, 2013.

R22: South Bronx, Wikipedia, the free encyclopedia, April 30, 2012.

R23: More Than Just Race: Being Black and Poor in the Inner City, Julius Wilson, W, W. Norton, New York, 2009.

R24:Essays, James Q. Wilson, **http://JQWilson.org** , June 24, 2014.

R25: R.I.'s Chance to Remake Schools, Ron Wolk, *Opinion*, Providence Journal, April 28, 2015.

R26: Bridges Out of Poverty, Ruby K. Payne, Philip E. DeVol, Terie Dreussi Smith, June 9, 2006.

R27: A Framework for Understanding Poverty, Ruby K. Paine, 4th Edition, May 15, 2005.

R28: School-within-a-school is a Waste, Carole Marshall, *Commentary*, Providence Journal, February 12, 2015.

R29: Stubborn Hope: Memoirs of an Urban Teacher, Carole Marshall, Create Space Publishing Platform, February 11, 2015.

R30: Inner City Gentrification Simulation Using hybrid Models of Cellular Automata and Multi-Agent Systems, Atsushi Nara, Paul M. Torrens, Department of Geography, University of Utah, {Gradual transformation from an impoverished community to one more affluent via restoration and upgrading [+ and -] includes a literature review of gentrification theories and a relevant methodology.}

R31: The Power Broker: Robert Moses and the Fall of New York City, Robert Caro, Alfred A. Knopf, 1974.

R32: Short-Term America, Michael T. Jacobs, Harvard Business School Press, Boston, 1991.

R33: Senator Bernie Sanders, Chairman, United States Committee on Veterans' Affairs, NBC's Meet the Press, September 14, 2014.

[R33A]: Senator Bernie Sanders, 2016 Presidential Candidate, NBC's Meet the Press, July 26, 2015.

R34: How Business Schools Can Help Reduce Inequality, Robert Reich, Harvard Business Review, September 12, 2014.

R35: The Price of Inequality, Joseph Stignitz, W.W. Norton & Company, 2012.

R36 Book Review: The Price of Inequality, John Case, August 10, 2012.

R37: Separate and Unequal, Thomas B. Edsall, Sunday Book Review New York Times, August 5, 2012.

R38: Book Review: The Price of Inequality, Chris Blackhurst, The Scotsman, August 18, 2012.

R39: The Great Divide: Unequal Societies and What We Can Do About Them, Joseph Stignitz, W.W. Norton & Company, April 20, 2015.

R40: The de-Valuing of America, The Fight for Our Culture and Our Children, William J. Bennett, Focus on the Family Publishing, Colorado Springs, Colorado, 1992.

R41: Book of Virtues, VI, VII, An Audio Library of Great Moral Stories, William j. Bennett, William Bennett, Elayne Bennett, Simon Schuster, New York, September 20, 2007.

R42: 50 Years Later, A Soul Struggles, Leonard Pitts, Miami Herald, May, 2011.

R43: Invisible Man, Ralph Ellison, Vintage Edition, 1952.

R44: Shadow and Act, Ralph Ellison, Vintage Edition, 1964

R45: Going to the Territory, Ralph Ellison, Vintage Edition, 1986.

R46: The Almanac of American Politics 1992, Michael Barone, Grant Ujifuse, January 1, 1991.

R47: References from the National Academies Press: Inner-City Poverty in the United States, Laurence E. Lynn, Jr., Michael G.H. McGeary, 1990; Ghetto Poverty and federal Policies and Programs, Michael G. H. McGeary; Family Structure, Poverty and the Underclass, Sara McLanahan, Irwin Garfinkel, Dorothy Watson, 1990.

R48 The Urban Poverty and Family Life Study, Joblessness and Urban Poverty Research Programs, Malcolm Wiener Center for Social Policy, 1987-1988.

R49: The Causes of Inner-City poverty: Eight Hypotheses in Search of Reality, Cityscape: A Journal of Policy Development and Research, Volume 3, Number 3, U.S. Department of Housing and Urban Development, Michael B. Teitz, Karen Chapple, 1998.

R50: Breaking the Cycle of Poverty in Young Families, National Human Services Assembly, Issue Brief, October, 2013.

R51: A New Model for Ending Inner City Poverty: An Interview with Ted Howard, Senior Fellow for Social Justice, Cleveland Foundation, by Neil Edington, Social Velocity, June 25, 2012.

R52: Social Solutions to Poverty: America's Struggle to Build a Just Society Scott-Myers and Charles Lemert, December, 2007.

R53: Health and Human Services Poverty Guidelines, United States Conference of Catholic Bishops, 2012.

R54 Readings, Lectures No. 1-23, MIT OpenCourseWare, Urban Studies Planning, Poverty, Public Policy and Controversy, Fall 2003.

R55 Paul Ryan's Approach to Poverty is Straight Out of the 19th Century, Arthur Delaney, Huffingtonpost.com, May 15, 2014.

R56: Paul Ryan's Immoral budget, CDF Action Alerts, Children's Defense Fund [CDF], Washington, DC, April, 2014.

R57: Http//budget.house.gov/expanding opportunity in America, Paul Ryan, July, 2014.

R58: Anti-poverty Activist Sister Simone, Rhode Island Could Be Petri-dish for Change, Tatiana Pina, Providence Journal, May 13, 2014.

R59: Core Indicators, The Annie E. Casey Foundation: 34% of Hispanic or Latino children lived in poverty in 2011.

R60: Rhode Island KIDS COUNT Factbook, 2012, 2013 Annual Publications.

R61: Paul Ryan's Immoral Budget, CDF Action Alerts, Children's Defense Fund, Washington, DC, April, 2014.

R62: Child Watch Column, Marian Wright Edelman, Children's Defense Fund, Washington, DC.

R63: It's All About Education: How Poverty Impacts Brain Development and Learning, Lauri Lee, GoLocalProvEducation Expert, April 29, 2015, http://m.golocalprov.com/lifestyle/its-all-about-education-how -poverty-impacts-brain-development-and-learning

R64: Adverse Childhood Experience [ACE], How Children Succeed, Paul Tough, Houghton Mifflin Harcourt, 2012.

R65: Chasing the Dream: Poverty and Opportunity in America, Dr. Kimberly Noble, Metrofocus, June 25, 2015.

R66: Protecting Children from Toxic Stress, David Bornstein, The Opinion Pages, New York Times, October 30, 2013.

R67: U.S. Poverty rises despite economic recovery, Economy, reporting by Lucia Mulikani, Caroline Hurner and Susan Heavey, edited by Mohammed Zargham, September 17, 2013.

R68: The High Moral and Economic Cost of Child Poverty in America, Marian Wright Edelman, Child Watch Column, Children's Defense Fund, September 19, 2014.

R69: Role of Parents, Michsel J. Meaney, James McGill Professor of Medicine at Douglas Mental Health University Institute of McGill University.

R70: Chicago Charter Schools: 1/3 better, 1/3 same, 1/3 worse, Chicago Tribune, Study: Charter Schools Lag Traditional Ones, October 13, 2014.

R71: National Center of Children in Poverty [NCCP], Mailman School of Public Health, Columbia University.

R72: Robert Pasternak, Senior Vice-President of Special Education for Voyager Learning Company, former Assistant Secretary for the Office Special Education and Rehabilitative Service [OSERS] at the U.S. Department of Education, speaking at the Rhode Island Association of School Principals Conference, August, 2007.

R73: Paul Sahlberg, Finnish Education Expert, speaking at the University of Rhode Island, Providence Journal, December 9, 2013.

R74: Thirty-five of Largest U.S. Cities Saw Increase in Child Poverty Rates between 2005-2013, Annie B. Casey Foundation, posted September 22, 2014.

R75: 2009 Kinsey Report, The Economic Impact of the Achievement Gap in America's Schools, McKinsey on Society, McKinsey & Company, April 2009. Also, Martin Gumpert, The Nation, Books and Ideas, March 25, 2009.

R76: Visible Learning: A Synthesis of Over 800 Meta-analyses Relating to Achievement Gap, John Hattie, 2009.

R77: Linking Childhood Trauma to Long-term Health and Social Consequences, ACE Study, On-going Collaborative Research between the Center for Disease Control [CDC] and Kaiser Permanente [HMO].

R78: How Children Succeed, Paul Tough, Houghton Mifflin Harcourt, 2012.

R79: The Effects of Poverty on Childhood Brain Development, Joan Luby, Andy Belden, Kelly Botteron, Natasha Marrus, Michael P. Harms, Casy Babb, Tomoyuki Nishino, Deanna Barch, JAMA, 2013.

R79a: On School Readiness, Where We Stand, National Association for the Education of Young Children, july, 1995.

R80: Primary School Readiness Assessment, posted in EDUCATION, Nadine, August, 2008.

R81: 3 Middle Grade Indicators of Readiness, Executive Summary, November, 2014.

R82: Middle Grades and the Transition to High School, University of Chicago, Consortium on Chicago School Readiness, The University of Chicago, 2015.

R83: Metrics for 'High School Readiness', Applied Survey Research, 2007.

R84: College Readiness: Education Week Webinar, Carole Adams, Contributing Writer, Education Week, College Readiness and Life Skills: Moving Beyond Academics, January 31, 2013.

R85: Redefining College Readiness, David T. Conley, Prepared for the Bill & Melissa Gates Foundation, March, 2007.

R86: What Is Employment Readiness, Employment Readiness Model, Valerie G. Ward Consultants Ltd., 2015.

R87: A Private Sector Model for Rebuilding Inner-City, Institute, December, 1998.

R88: Wholistic Ministry Model, Here's Life Inner City-New York, Cru Inner City NYC, 2012.

R89: New Hope for Solving America's Social Problems, Jay Ambrose, Providence Journal, October 14, 2014.

R90: Why government fails and what can we do about it, Lee H. Hamilton, Providence Journal, August 9, 2014.

R91: Parents Blast Hauppauge School Superintendent Over Placement of Homeless Students, http://hauppauge.patch.com, posted by Christine Sampson, Editor, September 18, 2013.

R92: Murdered Jewish civil rights workers to receive presidential medal, Haaretz, Jewish World News, November 12, 2014.

R93: Thanks to Four Bright Rainbows in Our National Cloud, Marian Wright Edelman's Child Watch Column, Children's Defense Fund, December 19, 2014.

R94: 1984 Democratic National Convention Keynote Address, Mario Matthew Cuomo, San Francisco, CA, July 16, 1984.

R95: Public can't expect politicians to solve all problems, Robert Whitcomb Commentary, Providence Journal, November 8, 2014.

R96: Criminalizing Poverty, Marion Wright Edelman's Child Watch Column, Children's Defense Fund, May 8, 2015.

R97: Investigation of the Ferguson Police Department, Civil Rights Division, United States Department of Justice, March 4, 2015.

R98: Attorney General Says Report on Ferguson Police Is 'Searing', Eliana Dockterman, [Eliana Dockterman@edockterman].

R99: Why Baltimore Burned, Todd Richissin, Patch National Staff April 29, 2015.

R100: What you really need to know about Baltimore, from a reporter who's lived there for over 30 years, Michael A. Fletcher, Washington Post, April 28, 2015.

R101: U.S. Launches Baltimore Police Investigation, Eric Tucker, The Associated press, Providence Journal, May 9, 2015.

R102: Social Crisis and Social Demoralization, {The Dynamics of Status In American Race Relations}, Ronald Kuykendall, Arissa Media Group, Portland, Oregon, 2005.

R103: Interview with the author of Social Crisis and Social Demoralization, Kam Williams, aalbc.com Site for African American Literature, May, 2015.

R104: W.E.B. DuBois, http://www. u-s-history.com/pages/h1613.html.

R105: The Talented Tenth, W.E.B.DuBois, The Negro Problem, September, 1903.

R106: The Talented Tenth [Excerpts], Gilder Lehrman, Yale University, May 26, 2015.

R107: Paul C. Taylor, NBC Evening News, June 19, 2015.

R108: Race: A Philosophical Introduction, Paul C. Taylor, Polity, May, 2013.

R109: Riots, anger could erupt here, Ray Hull, Providence Journal, May 7, 2015.

R110: Amazing Grace, Commentary, Providence Journal, June 29, 2015.

R111: Amazing Grace, Jonathan Kozol, Perennial, Crown Publishers, 1995.

R112: America-What Can We Do After Charleston? Marian Wright Edelman's Child Watch Column, Children's Defense Fund, July, 2013.

R113: America must solve race problem, Bob Houghtaling, Commentary, Providence Journal, May 8, 2015.

R114: George Bernard Shaw, Back to Methuselah, Act I, Selected Plays with Prefaces, vol. 2, p. 7, 1949,

R115: Free exchange, Reality Check, The Economist, October 17, 2015.

Authors' Biographies

ALBERT M. COLELLA, Ph.D. is a 1951 honor graduate from St. Raphael Academy in Pawtucket, RI and recipient of the Latin Medal there; he also played football for the 'Saints' earning Class A honors several times. He was also the recipient of a football scholarship to Rutgers University. While at Rutgers, he was drafted and is an U.S. Army veteran and a graduate of the Army's Leadership School. He received his BS Degree in Electrical Engineering from the University of Rhode Island in 1961; he also translated mathematical papers in French to English as part of his work-study program there. He also served as a mentor and tutor for his fellow students in several courses at URI but is better and humorously remembered for tutoring students in their challenging statistics class; all of whom received a grade of 'A' while he earned a 'B'. He entered government service at the United States Naval Underwater Ordnance Station at Newport, RI. pursuing graduate studies at the University of Rhode Island while working as a full-time Instrumentation Engineer and raising a family. He was awarded an MS Degree in Electrical Engineering [Control Systems] in 1965 and the PhD in Electrical Engineering [Nonlinear Adaptive Control Systems in 1973] from the University of Rhode Island.

In 1964, he took the position as Technical Assistant to the Laboratory Director for Control and Information Systems at NASA's Electronic Research Center. He was then appointed Technical Advisor to the Deputy Director of the Deep Submergence Rescue Vehicle

[DSRV] Program at MIT's Draper Laboratory in 1966. Program responsibility included technical program reviews and the assessment of guidance, control and display systems, laboratory real-time [man-in-the-loop] and computer simulations. He also served as a Guidance & Control Engineer with Raytheon's Missile Systems Division. In 1970, Dr. Colella served as the Technical Assistant to various program managers at the Transportation Systems Center of the United States Department of Transportation. In 1978, he returned to the United States Naval Undersea Warfare Center until his retirement in 1993 after 33 years of government service. This most recent assignment [lasting 25 years] involved the mathematical modeling of complex systems, expert system development, communications systems [where he teamed with members of the United States submarine fleet in the analysis of tactical communications]. In 1989, he served as Technical assistant to the Associate Director for Research and Technology. He was responsible for the conception, analysis and development of emerging technology assessment methodologies. He also served as Program Manager for the Center's Industrial Research & Development Program.

Upon his retirement in October of 1993, Dr. Colella was awarded membership in the 'Order of the Decibel' for his outstanding contributions and dedication in the areas of artificial intelligence and the mentoring of the Center's new professionals, and providing leadership in the Center's Industrial Research & Development Program. In particular, for his organization and management of the Center's IR&D Symposium with industry that became a model for the future of government and industrial interactions. It is important to note that this particular award is made selectively to retiring staff members who have contributed broadly and significantly to advancing the overall performance of the Center's mission.

Upon his retirement from government service, Dr. Colella extended his 30 years of teaching and mentoring within the government and, more formally, in both undergraduate and graduate programs [at various colleges and universities] and, then, by joining the faculty at the School of Technology at Johnson & Wales University. His areas of teaching there included all levels of mathematics, communications, robotics, artificial intelligence, instrumentation, control systems, systems analysis, modeling and simulation. His classes gave equal attention and emphasis to those skills needed to be successful in a specific technological area but, more importantly, to those skills [he always referred to them as the 'keys of life' that are needed to 'open doors' of opportunity] required for life success as an individual. In 1995, he was appointed as Head of the School of Technology and became the prime facilitator for upgrading all technology curricula and programs. He was principal advocate and mover for the integration of relevant areas of technology into ***all academic programs*** at the University.

During his 43 years of professional service, he became a mentor, advocate, facilitator, friend, confidant and, more often than not, a father-figure to myriad students and even some of the faculty. He always considered this particular role -- and family, community, government and military service -- as the most formative, meaningful and rewarding phases of his life. Whatever the arena, Dr. Colella always found a way [often creatively] to 'make a difference'. Once asked "Why?" about these roles, he simply replied that "Other people -- some unknown to me -- made a difference within my lifetime so why not 'pass it on' [aka 'paying it forward']. He was a walking and talking reminder that "Each of us really stand on the shoulders of others!" and "From those to whom much is given, much is expected!"

He has authored/co-authored more than 50 papers, articles, books, reports in his expertise and experienced areas of technology and management. He presented papers at a number of professional conferences where he sometimes received the 'best paper' award.

In parallel with his 43 years of professional activity, he was quite active in outreach and community service to those in need and, most importantly, being an advocate and mentor for his family, children and his 15 grandchildren. Some of these activities beyond the family included Big Brothers, advocate of teens within his faith community, Literacy Volunteers of America [LVA], Random Acts of Kindness, fund raising for families in need, home repair ministry and active supporter of Saint Raphael Academy where he served as scout for its football teams and was a founder of the Saints Club-an organization that was very much an advocate of the athletic programs in the 1950s, 1960s and 1970s. This latter activity was fueled by his awareness and appreciation that his years at Saint Raphael Academy were most formative for him. His outreach and community service activities were many but he always saw them as opportunities!

Additionally, he was the initiator, motivator and facilitator of efforts for addressing the needs of those in poverty and despair. His book with Steven Lippincott, ***Let's Start with the Children*** [published in 2013] relates the heart-breaking but also heart-warming and inspirational events of a 15 year ministry with the children and families of the challenging environment of the South Bronx in New York City. It was this ministry that was the inspiration for ***Let's Start with the Children*** which, in turn, became the inspirational force enabling the writing [with co-author, Joseph H. Crowley] and the publication of ***Poverty & Despair vs. Education & Opportunity***.

JOSEPH CROWLEY has lived the life. He grew up in a housing project, oldest of nine siblings whose father was an alcoholic and whose mother, while trying to do her very best, was overstressed in managing a home and nine children with little help from his father. His father worked as a fireman when doing so involved upwards of seventy hours per week in the fire station but would then, very often over the years, spend his off days and evenings in a bar. He is thankful to an aunt and an uncle who took interest in him and, today, understands the benefits of having caring adults in one's life.

Not having much parent supervision he was able to leave high school without a diploma. Fortunately, he was able to join the U.S. Air Force. A combination of maturation and being given considerable responsibility while in the service led to his desire for a college degree.

His first ambition was to be a history teacher but, with his less than stellar high school record, getting into a four year college was out of the question.

Having been exposed to computers while in the Air Force, this was early on in the use of computers, becoming a computer programmer looked like a good path. He was accepted into what was then Johnson & Wales Junior College -- on probation because of his high school record. Older and wiser, he graduated second in his class -- in high school he had been in the bottom five.

Within a year of beginning a career as a computer programmer/analyst, Joe had the opportunity to teach programming in a public career and technical high school. This led to more education where within five years, while teaching, he was able to earn a baccalaureate degree with high honors and an MBA -- being elected to two national honor societies.

He sees his transition from lacking a high school diploma to an MBA as reflecting the potential that might well be lost as children growing up in poverty environments try to overcome the barriers and find the bridges to work their way out. Inner city schools are loaded with Joes who might or might not break the bonds of poverty.

Over his career, Joe has served as teacher, assistant principal, principal, school district business manager, and, for a time, as an interim superintendent of schools. He has served as president of the Rhode Island Association of School Principals, president of the Mass. Association of School Business Managers, and chair of the New England Association of Schools and Colleges Commission on Technical and Career Institutions. He was also the executive director of the Rhode Island Association of School Principals serving on a number of education related boards and committees.

www.ingramcontent.com/pod-product-compliance
Lightning Source LLC
Chambersburg PA
CBHW072245270326
41930CB00010B/2269